IAN R. MITCHELL is an historian, who gave up teaching to devote himself to writing full time. After graduating from university in his native Aberdeen in 1973, Ian did postgraduate research at Leeds, followed by a British Council scholarship to study in Berlin. The author of articles in learned journals, and of a standard textbook on Bismarck, Ian taught for over 20 years at Clydebank College, mainly on German history. Increasingly interested in Scottish history and heritage, and a lifelong hillwalker, Ian has produced several other books, including *Scotland's Mountains before the Mountaineers*, a pre-history of explorations and ascents in the Scottish mountains. Ian also writes frequently on outdoor matters for climbing journals and the general media. In addition, he gives talks and slide shows on his books, including this one.

By the Same Author:

Bismarck (Holmes McDougall, 1980)

Mountain Days and Bothy Nights (Luath Press, 1988) with Dave Brown

The First Munroist (The Ernest Press, 1993) with Pete Drummond

Second Man on the Rope (Mercat Press, 1995)

Mountain Footfalls (Mercat Press, 1996)

The Mountain Weeps (Stobcross Press, 1997)

Scotland's Mountains Before the Mountaineers (Luath Press, 1998)

On the Trail of Queen Victoria in the Highlands (Luath Press, 2000)

Mountain Outlaw (Luath Press, 2003)

This City Now: Glasgow and its working class past (Luath Press, 2005)

A View from the Ridge (Luath Press, 2007) with Dave Brown

Walking Through Scotland's History

Two Thousand Years on Foot

IAN R. MITCHELL

Luath Press Limited

EDINBURGH

www.luath.co.uk

First Published 2001
by National Museums of Scotland Publishing Ltd.

This edition 2007
Reprinted 2008
Reprinted 2009

ISBN: 978-1-905222-44-5

The paper used in this book is recyclable. It is made from low
chlorine pulps produced in a low energy, low emission manner
from renewable forests.

Printed and bound by
Bell & Bain Ltd., Glasgow

Map by Jim Lewis

Typeset in 10.5 point Sabon by
3btype.com

For Manda, who taught me to walk

Acknowledgements

I would like to thank the following: Lawrence Keppie of the Hunterian Museum in Glasgow, for a fascinating telephone conversation on the footwear of Roman legionaries; Bruce Lenman who modified some of my over-forceful arguments on the Jacobites; Irvine Butterfield who made available to me his research on whisky smuggling; Angus Mackenzie who shared his reminiscences of the Hielandman's Umbrella and the life of Glasgow Gaels of the 1930s; my parents, Robert Mitchell and Jessie Henderson, who discussed memories of 'wakkin the matt' in Aberdeen; Tom Williamson, who brought to my attention the unemployed workers' tramp to Kinlochleven in the 1930s; and Bill McQueen of the Carbeth Hutters' campaign.

Note to the Second Edition

For this new edition of *Walking through Scotland's History*, I have added two walk descriptions to each chapter, hoping thus to encourage more readers to get out from their armchairs and onto their feet. It should be stressed that for each walk the cited os map, as well as suitable walking equipment, is necessary.

Contents

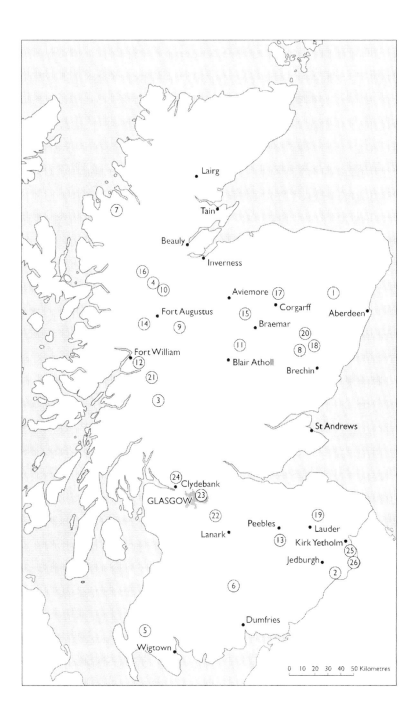

Introduction

WALKING UPRIGHT SHARES WITH speech the distinction of being the only truly human activity. Just as (despite having communication tools and patterns) no other animal has developed speech as distinguished from a range of sounds, so no animal can approximate to walking on two legs, other than as a short-lived stumble. *Homo erectus* took a step away from our simian ancestors, and in time emerged *Homo sapiens*, a walking, thinking creature, unique, for good or ill, in nature. On a basic level we still recognise this far along the evolutionary scale – what other developments delight a parent as much as their offspring's first words and first steps?

Walking has been such an essential part of human life and society that it should hardly need pointing out. However, in bookshops 'Walking' is classed as a leisure activity, and for most people in Western industrialised societies walking has become divorced from the general process of living and working. If it is engaged in at all, walking takes the form of a weekend pursuit in the countryside, something tacked on to the business of normal living. Moreover, it is clear that for most people, walking is not even this. Figures suggest that half the population never takes any exercise which results in sweating or quickness of breathing, which indicates that for millions of people, walking consists of no more than a trip from the house to the garage.

This book will attempt to give a description of a world we have lost, and though of necessity concentrating on Scotland, I am sure that its contents could be replicated for any modern society. It shows that, with few exceptions, before the era of the steam engine and later the internal combustion engine, most human activities were carried out through the medium of walking. Walking through Scotland's history we discover that the country was conquered in part by walking Roman legions. Those who brought Christianity to Scotland did so on foot, and were later followed by pedestrian pilgrims. Apart from their mounted minority, the armies of the Jacobite rebellions marched, and later scientists and cartographers who studied and mapped the country used Shanks's pony by and large.

Not only did Scotland's cattle walk to market, but their drovers did too, and a century ago seasonal workers in the fishing industry and agriculture walked to and from their places of employment, as did, until much more recent times, the tinkers to be found on the highways. The move to an urban society did not immediately end all this pedestrian activity, and people often continued to walk to work and to church in the cities, and in their new environment began to develop novel forms of walking linked to social and courtship rituals.

In presenting this account of walking in the past, I make an appeal for the claim of walking in the present. There is no doubt that walking is the single most beneficial human activity. Research shows that walking enhances emotional well-being, and that if more people walked, levels of bronchial, heart and other diseases would decline. The decrease in the usage of the motor car brought about by an increase in leg usage would help curb atmospheric pollution. And people can always start walking now, without any investment other than time. Walking also has the advantage that you can keep at it till the end of your life, unlike some other forms of exercise.

Walking need not involve mountaineering, with which it is often associated. A larger variety of walking options exists, from following pilgrims' trails and those of the drovers, to walking on canal tracks laid down by navvies, or pounding urban trails in the Glasgow Gaels' footsteps. The stimulation – not only visual, but also social and historical – brought about by the rich varieties of walking on offer, can help to re-enforce the link between walking and thinking that makes us human. Walking is also a democratic activity in which almost all can take part in a non-competitive way, each taking from it according to their needs, and participating according to their abilities.

Restrictions of space made this book shorter than I would have liked. So here I make my apologies to all those who were omitted. Some are well known, and there exist accessible accounts of their walking – such as James Hogg, the Ettrick Shepherd, who tramped hundreds of miles through the West Highlands looking for a sheep farm in the 1800s. But others are known only to their descendants – such as Ninian Lockhart, who walked to London from Kirkcaldy in Fife to demand an improvement in the terms of his lease from the laird of the Raith estate, and got it; Alexander Beck of Thornhill, who walked 15 miles each way, each day, to work underground at the pit at Kirkconnel; John Mackenzie, who tramped from Kirriemuir to Forres in 1881 through the Cairngorms to start a new ironmonger's shop; and McHardy, the Corgarff piper, who (after a day in the fields) would walk to Tomintoul or Ballater to play at some celebration, and walk back through the night to begin work again the next day. These, and many other examples of remarkable walking feats which people enthusiastically supplied me with, were often so unique that they were impossible to fit into any thematic chapters.

I hope my book gives enough examples of the various

epochs of Scottish history though which people walked to be of interest, and also stimulates readers to follow in at least some of the footsteps it describes. Every journey begins with the first steps, just as every book starts with a few words.

CHAPTER I

The Roman Legions

THEY WALKED, or rather marched, into Caledonia. They went on foot to meet the enemy. When they held a part of what is now Scotland, they patrolled it on foot – and they marched back out again when the occupation was over. The Roman legions were not the first people to walk through Scottish history, but they are the first of whom we have written and archeological records of their passing.

By the time Gnaeus Julius Agricola (40–93AD) arrived in Britain as Governor in 77AD, most of central and southern England was under Roman rule; lightning campaigns in north Wales and northern England brought him to the territory of present-day Scotland, and a full-scale invasion was launched in 79AD. Much of what we know of this invasion comes from the biography, *The Agricola*, written by the general's son-in-law, Cornelius Tacitus.

The Roman invasion force amounted to four legions, a little short of 20,000 men. Cavalry was a much smaller element, with 3,000 men. So while some rode into Scotland, and some, like the officers, were doubtless carried, the vast majority walked over the Southern Uplands to the line of the Forth in 79AD, meeting little resistance. Their scouts, or *exploratores*, had gone ahead of the army, and either found the obvious lines of geographical access into Scotland for themselves, or discovered that rough-trodden roads of a sort existed already, for the invasion lines appear to have been pretty close to the present M74 and A68 roads! The legionaries were equipped with iron cuirasses, bronze or iron helmets, and a curving rectangular shield, as well as swords, daggers and javelins. Whilst these offered protection against the enemy, they offered little defence against the Scottish weather.

After consolidating his grip on southern Scotland by building forts, Agricola marched onwards in 82AD, through Strathmore, to hunt out the elusive Caledonians (the name under which the various tribes of the north were grouped). According to Tacitus, the Caledonians had red hair, and he thought they were of Germanic origin. The Caledonians initially followed the correct strategy of retreating from the Romans, causing Agricola to call them 'a pack of spiritless cowards', and indulging in the occasional surprise raid – one of which almost led to a disaster, with a night attack on the camp of the Ninth Legion.

That year and the next the Roman legionaries route-marched through the cold and barren territory of the Taexali tribe in present-day Angus, the Vacomagi in what is now Aberdeenshire, and the Boresti, who possibly inhabited Moray. Walking 15 and sometimes up to 25 miles in a day, they built a temporary fortified camp after each day's march. This involved digging a defensive ditch and latrines, and setting up leather tents held by wooden pegs under which they slept. As well as the ferocious climate, the soldiers had to deal with ground of extreme difficulty – bogs and rocks abounded, and there can have been few (if any) paths, never mind roads, as they advanced further into Caledonian territory.

Tacitus' account is vague and can be interpreted to mean the Romans reached 'the furthest limit of Britain', which would have been Caithness. Since the Roman fleet sailed round the Orkney Islands, it would perhaps be wise not to dismiss this claim over-readily. Ptolemy's map of Britain, circa 140AD, probably compiled from accounts of Agricola's campaign, shows knowledge of the geography and tribal territories of Scotland far beyond the areas in which Roman remains have been discovered so far. Evidence of a line of Roman camps situated about a day's marching distance apart indicates that the Romans advanced through Strathmore and present-day Kincardineshire, and then across the Rivers Dee and Don in the North East, reaching as far as Moray ('Pinnata Castra' in Ptolemy has been tentatively identified as Burghead) – and they most probably walked even further. (It is tempting to argue that these camps belonged to Agricola's actual march, but they may date from later.) Part of this country was crossed and re-crossed several times before Agricola heard that the Caledonians had rather foolishly assembled a huge army at a place Tacitus calls 'Mons Graupius', and he hastened there to give them battle.

According to Tacitus, around 30,000 Caledonians had assembled under their leader Calgacus at Mons Graupius, which many modern authorities equate with the hill of Bennachie in Aberdeenshire. The person of 'Calgacus', which simply means 'swordsman', may be an invention of Tacitus, as may be his stirring speech to the assembled Caledonians before the battle – one wonders how any of the Romans could have heard or understood it:

> We, the most distant dwellers on earth, the last of the free, have been shielded till today... Pillagers of the world, the Romans have exhausted the land... A rich enemy excites their cupidity, a poor one their lust for power... To robbery, butchery and rapine, they give the lying name of 'government'; they create a desolation and they call it peace.

If he existed, Calgacus was a better rhetorician than a general, for having decided to meet the Romans in a set battle, he threw away the defensive advantage of his position and the Caledonian troops began to advance downhill, exposing themselves to the Roman cavalry. The battle turned into a rout and the Roman losses were light at under 400 men. The Caledonians, according to Tacitus, lost some 10,000 men, and the Roman legionaries' arms ached with the slaughter.

Agricola marched northwards to the Moray Firth, over-awing the tribes and taking hostages, before retiring to Inchtuthil, near present-day Perth, for the winter. Though he had won the battle, Agricola had seen that it would be a huge effort for Rome to conquer and annex the vast, inhospitable territory of northern Scotland – 'nothing but waves and rocks', according to Tacitus' rendering of Calgacus' speech – and only a couple of years after Mons Graupius, Roman troops were withdrawn to the Forth-Clyde line. On and behind that line they were to remain for about 80 years (excluding a temporary retreat to Hadrian's Wall circa 120–140AD), and we must assume that it was in this period that the Roman roads were constructed in Scotland.

While the existence of the Antonine Wall, constructed in the 140s AD, and its associated forts is fairly well known, it is less appreciated that Scotland has over 500 miles of Roman roads. They were the first roads in Scotland to be deliberately constructed as far as is known, and were amongst the best for almost 1,500 years, until the Hanoverian military roads were laid down. The main military arteries were: from the Cheviots to the Tweed at Melrose and then on to the Forth; from the Solway to Annandale and north to the Lower Clyde; and from the wall at Camelon near present-day Falkirk, north to the Tay and possibly further.

Additionally there was the Military Way, a road which ran behind the rampart of the Antonine Wall, and other connecting roads elsewhere. These roads, given the frontier nature of Scotland's occupation, were not of the quality of roads in other parts of the Empire, which were fully Romanised and integrated politically and economically. But they were well constructed – a section of the Annandale road, for example, is over six metres wide and has a foundation of 28 centimetres of large stones, with 10 centimetres of smaller stones on top. Few of the roads in Scotland were paved, unlike in areas of more permanent conquest. North of the Antonine Wall, the road crossed the Forth to the camp at Ardoch and beyond, probably deteriorating as it went.

These roads would have made the job of the foot-slogging legionary a little easier, whether he was on routine route marches south of the wall to maintain his military prepared-ness, or on more dangerous expeditions to the forts and watchtowers which lay to the north, in territory imperfectly conquered. And let us not forget that by and large it was the legionaries themselves who had built the roads, possibly supplemented by local slave labour. Like General Wade's soldiers 1,500 years later, the legionaries made their own ways. The Roman roads we know were marked by milestones, just as the Antonine Wall was marked by distance slabs com-memorating the building of sections by the various legions. Surprisingly, so far only one such milestone has been found, at Ingliston in West Lothian.

Something which appears to have made walking through Scotland less unpleasant for the Roman legionaries was a series of developments in their footwear design. Roman legionaries wore leather shoes, much like modern sandals, which were laced up and tied round the heel. In the pleasant climes of much of the Empire, and with good roads, these doubtless frequently wore out but would have sufficed. In Scotland, with harsher conditions, the sandals were made larger, almost like boots, presumably for warmth and support, and were laced higher up the leg. The underside of the legionaries' shoes were made of composited layers of leather which formed a sole, and into these soles iron studs were driven and then folded over inside the shoe – the soles of the legionaries' feet must have been pretty hardened, as they wore no protective socks. Replacement footwear was one of the most frequent needs of the legions, and at Bar Hill Fort rubbish tip over 500 items of all sizes of footwear were found after almost 2,000 years.

Men engaged in such walking feats needed to be well fed and housed. The larger forts were equipped with a hospital, and also bath houses like the ones at Bearsden and Bothwellhaugh, where soldiers could relax in comfort. The diet of the soldiers was a fortifying one. Middens show not only grain, but cheese, fruit, nuts, fish and a variety of meat including mutton, beef and wild boar. It is hardly surprising that many natives actually joined the auxiliary legions due to the attractions of the legionarie's life. Often serving in the same place for a period of 25 years, many legionaries formed associations with local women; thus to the Caledonians' genetic stock was added the blood of Batavians and Tungrians (from Germany and Belgium), as well as that of Thracians (from present-day Bulgaria).

The Romans abandoned the Antonine Wall in the decade 160–170AD, destroying their camps, filling in wells and evacuating by the roads which they themselves had built. A few forts were maintained to the north till about 180AD, and then they too were abandoned – it looked as if the Romans had left Scotland for good. But then, in 208AD, the Emperor Septimius Severus advanced from Hadrian's Wall with a massive force of 40,000 men, to engage the Maetae and the Caledonians 'who lived beyond them' in battle. Severus advanced, probably partly along old Roman roads and using former camps, 'almost to the end of the island', suffering heavy casualties but imposing a peace treaty on the native tribes. He took the title 'Britannicus', conqueror of Britain, but a year after his expedition there was a serious revolt; though this was crushed it showed the difficulties of holding northern Britain, and no real gain of territory was made. Basically Scotland held nothing that the Romans wanted. Severus had achieved military glory and strengthened his position in Rome, but he, like other Romans by this time, knew that Caledonia was not worth the bother of conquering – it was no valuable prize. Severus' expedition is likely to have followed the route of Agricola's; though, as previously mentioned, tentative Roman sites have been identified as far as the Moray Firth, none have yet been found beyond that.

Soon the tide turned, and an overstretched Rome faced increasing incursions into its British territory from north of Hadrian's Wall. These intruders also walked, some several hundred miles, in their pillaging. Among the intruders was a group of people called 'Picti' (Picts) by a Roman poet in 297AD. In 306AD an expedition under Constantius Chlorus advanced north and defeated the 'Caledonians and other Picts', possibly south of the actual wall itself, but it was only a temporary respite. Effectively the Romans had walked out of Scottish history with the retreat of Severus in 211AD, leaving very little behind, even in terms of place names. One cannot imagine however, as they walked away from Scotland, that many of the countless thousands of legionaries who had served their time there were especially sorry to see the back of the country they had partially conquered – and held – on foot. The roads which the Romans left behind them gradually decayed from lack of maintenance, but while most were to disappear or become overgrown, some of them were used for a purpose much different from that of the people who had originally built them.

Suggested Walks

WALK 1

Bennachie, the Mither Tap (OS 38)

This hill, the probable Mons Graupius of Tacitus' narrative, is an accessible and easy ascent. Its present name is derived from Gaelic, meaning 'Hill of the Breasts' from the many granite tors on its plateau. The most interesting of these, though not the highest, is the Mither Tap (Mother Top), upon which is located the neolithic fort.

Start at the car park at Tullos, east of the hill. Nearby at Esson's Croft there are remains of squatters' cottages from the 19th century: they seized land here when the common lands were appropriated by local landowners. Take the way-marked trail through delightful mixed woodland till it emerges onto the moor and ascends through the double wall of the fort to the summit (518 m). Carrying on across the plateau leads to the highest point, Oxen Craig at 528 m. The return can be varied by descending the Maiden Causeway to Pittodrie House Hotel, and then taking the good track due south along the wood's edge to the car park.

Return trip to Mither Tap: 3 miles, 2 hours; full outing 8 miles, 4–5 hours.

WALK 2

Dere Street (OS 70 and 80)

Dere Street was the main Roman road into Scotland, running from the Tyne to the Forth. The best walkable section from Jedburgh to Rochester covers 21 miles. This is a wonderful walk over easy angled terrain on mostly grassy tracks. The description given here covers the route from Jedburgh to the Scottish border.

Start about 2 miles north of Jedburgh, on the A698 on the east bank of the Jed River. Dere Street runs south-east to the Roman camp at Cappuck and continues past Shibden Hill and Whitton Edge (about a mile and a half here is on the public road). Then the route turns south gaining height over the shoulder of Hare Law and attaining its maximum height of over 300 m, before descending past the Roman camp at Pennymuir. You can arrange a pick-up here at Tow Ford, or continue further.

From Tow Ford (a real ford) the road climbs steeply towards Blackhall Hill, along what is probably the best preserved part of the road, a broad grassy sward, and follows the border past the faint remains of a Roman signal station to the impressive remains of the camp at Chew Green (just in England). From thence the way can be traced back west down Whiteside Hill to the end of the public road at Hindhope where hopefully transport has been arranged. (Your driver gets there by Morebattle and Hownam.) Or retrace steps back along Dere Street itself from Chew Green.

Distance to Tow Ford: 9 miles, 4 hours. Hindhope by Chew Green: 15 miles, 8 hours.

CHAPTER 2

The Christian Missionaries

AFTER THE WITHDRAWAL of the Roman legions, the pedestrian baton was taken from the men of war by men of peace, and the early Christian missionaries walked round a much greater part of Scotland than the legionaries had been able to, and with a more enduring impact. Undertaken in a time of warfare and lawlessness, their journeys were remarkable, and some who made them paid the ultimate price of martyrdom.

An early miraculous walker was St Ninian, who was probably born in Galloway about 360AD, and was a Roman citizen. In his youth he reputedly walked to Rome, and there met Pope Damasus. His journey was undertaken on the good Roman roads. Upon his return he founded a monastery called Candida Casa at Whithorn on Wigtown Bay, and after its completion in 397AD he evangelised widely. He apparently visited Cumberland and Westmoreland, while places in Kirkcudbrightshire (St Ringan's Cave) and Ayrshire (St Ninian's Well) record his presence there. He went on a mission to the Southern Picts, and probably reached Aberdeenshire, where there is another St Ninian's Well. All of these journeys would have been accomplished on foot, though if St Ninian's Isle on Shetland records his presence, that archipelago must have been attained by sea. In some of the territory he evangelised, Ninian would have been aided by the various Roman roads which existed, for example in southern Scotland, but elsewhere faint tracks through the woods and mosses would have been all he had to follow.

Consider St Columba, and the tales of his 6th century wanderings given in St Adamnan's *Life of Saint Columba*. In 565AD, two years after arriving on Iona, Columba travelled via the Great Glen, where he saw a monster in Loch Ness, to present-day Inverness. His route is marked by place names like 'Kilcolmkull' at Benderloch, 'Eilean Columbkill' at the mouth of Loch Arkaig, and 'Clachan Chollumchille' at Invermoriston. At Inverness, Columba converted King Brude to Christianity. Further to this he visited, amongst other places, the island of Skye – although that could well have been by boat from Iona. 'Loch Chollumkille' in Trotternish, now drained, records his passing. At Iona the monks went about their business of prayer and study, as well as attending to the work of agriculture, barefoot. For a long journey they allowed themselves the indulgence of simple sandals. When we imagine the territory that was being walked through – no Roman roads to help here – these missions of Columba are great feats of endurance over fatigue and pain.

The hard and simple life of the monks appears to have made them physically resilient. St Kentigern, or Mungo (514–601AD), always slept on stone, with a rock for a pillow, and his diet of bread, milk, cheese and butter would have provided the carbohydrates and protein necessary for long walking feats. Expelled from Strathclyde by a pagan king, Kentigern walked south through the Lake District, where he 'preached to the pagans in the mountains', and eventually arrived at Menovia in South Wales, establishing a monastery at Llanelly. Unexpectedly called back to 'Glaschu' in his old age by King Redderech, he walked as far as Dumfriesshire, where he was met by the king – and possibly given a lift for the last part of his journey. Most of these southward walks would have been made on Roman roads before they decayed, but not his latter-day missions to such places as Upper Deeside, where he visited Glen Gairn – and where at Abergairn there used to be a St Mungo's Fair. Try imagining these journeys in the foul weather which so often prevails on our island, with footwear of a thin sockless sandal, and dressed in a hair shirt and goat-skin coat. Mungo and others like him would have needed their pastoral staff as much for physical support as for spiritual authority.

Another formidable pedestrian was St Adamnan, who succeeded to Columba's post on Iona. In 686AD he took part in a mission from Iona to Northumberland, landing at the Solway and walking across the moors to the east coast, probably along the old Roman military way. Legend also has it that St Adamnan took the classic missionary route from Ireland, sailing up Glen Etive and crossing the mountains to near present-day Bridge of Orchy. He then wended his way eastwards through the mountains to Glen Lyon. Adamnan lived in the latter glen, where there is a 'Magh Eonan' (Adamnan's Plain), and he is probably buried at 'Milton Eonan', where he is reputed to have established a mill (Baile a' mhuillin Eonan) and restored a church. Apparently he decided on this place because at that juncture in his journey the thong on his sandal broke and he was temporarily immobilised, which he took as a sign. Until it stopped working, the mill kept Adamnan's festival day, 6 October, as a holiday.

En route through to Glen Lyon in Auch Glen, there is a Celtic chapel and burial ground at the Allt-na-h-Annait, which flows off Beinn Dorain. Here too is found Beinn Mhanach (3,125 ft), 'the Hill of the Monk', but which monk? Is the hill named in honour of Adamnan, who passed beneath it, as a landmark between Glen Lyon and Glen Orchy? Or is it named after the monks who kept their long and lonely watch in the glen at its foot – or even possibly cold vigil on its summit?

Difficult as things were for missionaries at this time in southern Scotland and the central Highlands, they were much more perilous further north, where conditions of greater lawlessness prevailed, the terrain was harder, and ecclesiastical institutions were more scattered. St Donan was an Irish missionary who came to Candida Casa and who, from circa 580AD, evangelised in Wigtownshire and Ayrshire, where 'Kildonan' and 'Cairn Donnan' commemorate him. Walking north, possibly via the Great Glen, he and his followers stopped near present-day Helmsdale, and at the Strath of Kildonan established a monastic settlement, from whence they evangelised as far as Buchan, where Donnan's Fair used to be held near Auchterless. Viking raids made things impossible at Helmsdale, so Donan and his followers set off on foot again, tracing a route in all likelihood back down the Great Glen and through Glengarry to Kintail and Skye, whence they sailed to Eigg and established another settlement. This did not protect them, and in 617AD Donan and 52 of his followers were massacred on Eigg by pirates.

Martyrdom too was the fate of St Maelrubha, who was slain by Danish pirates at Strathnaver on 21 April 722AD. He had come a long way from home, sailing from Ulster where he was born in 642AD, first to Kintyre, and then up the west coast to Applecross (Apurcrossan) with his followers, where he established a sanctuary (a'Chomraich) under his rule, six miles in all directions, marked by boundary stones. He evangelised the local area and further afield to Loch Maree, where a chapel was established on 'Eilean Mairui' (whose remains are still visible). 'Kilmarui' in Bracadale on Skye commemorates a visit by him or his followers. However, his wanderings even took him as far as the east coast, where his passing, or those of his disciples, is commemorated in the Sammarive's Fairs, formerly held in Forres, Keith and Fordyce, near Portsoy. These journeys were huge pedestrian undertakings, and Maelrubha seems to have approached the east coast via Kinlochewe, Achnasheen and Garve, for this is given as the route he followed on the more fateful mission northwards, which continued through Strath Oykell to Strathnaver, where he met his death. How imperfectly Maelrubha had christianised the natives is shown by the survival of various pagan practices in the Applecross area. Bulls were sacrificed to the god Mourie, a practice forbidden by the local presbytery as late as 1656.

Things were more politically stable by the time our last great missionary walker, St Duthac, appeared on the scene. Scotland had become a more united country, and Christianity had a much firmer footing in the land. Duthac was born in Tain, formerly known as 'Baile-Dhuich', and his name is widely commemorated in the region. As Bishop of Rosshire, Duthac was interred at Tain after his death in 1065. However, his missionary zeal gave his mark to Scottish topography around all points of the compass from Tain. In the North East there is 'Kilduthie' in former Kincardineshire, while further south in Fife is 'Baldutho' (Duthac's Town). To the north he wandered as far as Wick, where a remote chapel in the Flow of Kiminster is named after him. 'St Dudoch's Kirk' is accompanied by several other enclosures and a possible garden and graveyard, and for many centuries the local people laid offerings of bread, cheese and silver at the establishment.

Duthac had been educated in Ireland, and it is likely that the westward route associated with the saint was the one he took when travelling to and from there. However, it may have simply been his duties as bishop which took him from Easter Ross to the west coast at Kintail, where 'Loch Duich' is named after him, and where at 'Kilduich' he built a church. His route between these two coastal points is indicated by the map – 'Cadha Dhubhthaich' (Duthac's Pass) lies between Kintail and Glen Affric; and across the pass, which attains a height of almost 1,800 ft, and down that glen towards Tain, lies 'the Clergyman's Route', which is today followed by hundreds of walkers. Let them try it in thin sandals and a hair shirt, and without the road, which turns into a Land Rover track and then a good path, existing there today. Duthac was so revered in his lifetime and afterwards that Tain became a place of pilgrimage after his death, visited even by kings.

We can say that the peregrinations of these missionaries among the mountains gave the collective consciousness of the Celtic Church based on Iona (and the other Churches operating in Scotland at this time) a detailed mental map of the country. And a mental map it must have been – never written down, and relying on instructions based on physical features and places named by, or often after, the saints themselves. And these journeys appear to have been made almost entirely on foot. The missionaries walked... but did they climb the hills?

Since Moses descended from Mount Sinai with the Ten Commandments, there has been an association between mountains and Christian spirituality. Mountain tops give space for divine meditation, and in pre-scientific days the summits would have been assumed to reach closer to Heaven. Some of the early Scottish saints did, at least, ascend modest summits. St Fillan, active in the 8th century, came from Ireland to the Central Highlands where his name is littered, focusing on 'Strath Fillan' itself, where lies Saint Fillan's Chapel. On top of 'Dunfillan', near Comrie, is St Fillan's Chair, where the saint went to fast and pray, though this hill is only a modest 600 ft. In his wanderings St Fillan reputedly only ate one day in four, as penance for sin.

In the same area of Perthshire associated with St Fillan there is a tale of St Cuthbert, whose *Life* records the following interesting case, showing the link between mountain tops and spirituality:

> He began to dwell in different parts of the country, and coming to a town called Dul forsook the world and became a solitary. No more than a mile from the town is a high and steep mountain called by the inhabitants Doilweme, and on its summit he began to lead a solitary life.

In the tale, Cuthbert's quiet life of prayer and mortification was interrupted when the daughter of a local Pictish chief accused him of violating her, so the good saint had the earth open and swallow her up! Weem Hill (1,638 ft) may be a candidate for the mountain in question. Cuthbert has the honour of having a long-distance walk, St Cuthbert's Way, named after him. It commemorates the route he took from Melrose to Lindisfarne, where he spent many years in incredible self-mortification before his death in 687AD.

The region of Breadalbane has a few saintly mountain names. Directly north of St Fillan's Chapel lies 'Beinn Chaluim', 3,354 ft, which some authorities believe is named after Columba himself. But this indicates part of our problem – places may be named *in honour* of a saint, rather than as a record of their presence there, for there is no note of

Columba ever having been in this area. But is it too far fetched to suggest that the mountain was a spiritual retreat for the monks at St Fillan's Chapel? Given their walking feats, the ascent of the bens would not have been beyond the physical capabilities of the early Christian missionaries.

Suggested Walks

WALK 3

Adamnan's Way: Auch Glen and Bheinn Mhanach (OS 50 and 51)

St Adamnan had already sailed a long way from Ireland, and probably up Loch Etive and then walked over the mountains, by the time he reached the entrance to Auch Glen, which he took through to his final resting place in Glen Lyon. From the A82 road follow the route past Auch farm (once tenanted by Rob Roy) and under the massive viaduct of the West Highland railway, then up Auch Glen where a Land Rover track today replaces the faint path the saint would have followed. The Allt na h-Annait burn flows into the Allt Kinglass after a couple of miles, and here can be seen a large square enclosure, whose low walls are still visible. This was the site of a Celtic monastic settlement which dates from even before Adamnan's journeys in the 7th century. The settlement probably gave its name to Bheinn Mhanach (Monk's Mountain), which can easiest be climbed from the watershed between the Allt a Chuirn and Strath Tarabhan. Long grassy slopes lead to the summit of the mountain.

It is possible to continue Adamnan's route along the northern shores of Glen Lyon. At first this is rough, but eventually at Gleann Meran a bulldozed road is reached which leads to the east end of the loch. Here the hydro dam announces the start of the public road. From there it is a further 10 miles to Milton Eonan, but only the most dedicated walkers would instruct their lift to be waiting there, rather than at Pubil.

Round trip to summit of Bheinn Mhanach: 11 miles, 6 hours; from Auch to Pubil: 14 miles, 7 hours.

WALK 4
St Duthac's Way: Affric to Kintail (os 25 and 33)

By the time he arrived at the eastern end of Loch Affric, St Duthac would already have been footsore from the many miles he had walked from Tain. We will retrace the later part of his route, itself a hard enough walk even today.

You should arrange drop off at the car park a mile east of Affric Lodge, and take the old drove road north of Loch Affric, not the horrible bulldozed Land Rover track on its southern shore. After four or so miles this joins the route which carries on further west towards Alltbeithe Youth Hostel, past many old ruins from the Clearance times. Thence most walking traffic now continues on a route south-west down Fionngleann towards Kintail, which later became one of the main east-west drove roads. But the saint's route went to the north of Bheinn Fhada (the aptly-named Long Mountain), and through the pass now known as Bealaich an Sgairne, formerly Cadha Duthac (Duthac's Pass), where there is a Duthac's Well (Topar Dhuich). This pass reaches a height of over 500 m, before descending down Strath Croe to Loch Duich, (Duthac's Loch). Here the weary saint would undoubtedly have found a boat, and you can pick up a bus back to Fort William, or onwards to Skye. While waiting, examine the gravestones in the ruined church by the loch. One of them is of the illicit distiller Hamish (Dhu) Macrae, mentioned in Chapter Nine.

Affric to Kintail: 17 miles, 9–10 hours, or overnight at Allbeithe Youth Hostel.

CHAPTER 3

Medieval Pilgrims

THE JOURNEYS OF MEDIEVAL PILGRIMS were very different from the arduous wanderings of the saints and holy men and women whom they were commemorating. Indeed, the pilgrimages were highly organised commercial phenomena, resembling as much a modern package holiday as a penance. The avowed purpose of a pilgrimage was to obtain remission for sin, and the successful pilgrim could expect to shorten his or her time in Purgatory, or even go straight to Heaven, provided the penance was carried out properly. The requisite amount was also to be paid in the form of donations to, and purchases of indulgences from, the Church.

For the pilgrim, the belief was that the saints could converse with God and do some plea bargaining for the sinner. Spending a good part of one's life savings would have seemed worthwhile to shorten the terrors and torments of the afterlife. But an undoubted attraction of the pilgrimage would also have been its holiday aspect, and the relief offered thereby from the world of labour and monotony which many people endured. If Chaucer's *Canterbury Tales* are anything to go by, the pilgrimage was as much about meeting new people, seeing new places and telling tales, as anything else. There is little of self-mortification in his account of pilgrims en route to Canterbury.

For the rich, pilgrimage was a not infrequent activity, both at home and abroad. Richer pilgrims would have gone further and more often than poorer ones. There are many accounts of Scots undertaking pilgrimages in England and to Rome itself and at a grave on the Isle of May in Fife, a buried pilgrim even has a scallop shell in his mouth, to show that he had been to Santiago in Spain (thus ensuring a speedier unlocking of Heaven's door). For the middling or poorer sort, a pilgrimage would have been a once in a lifetime experience, and it is hard to imagine that the lowest stratum in medieval society, the serfs, would have been able to afford the expense of a pilgrimage at all. Since, with other factors, remission of sin was in proportion to distance travelled and money given over to the Church, it was easier in Catholic Europe for the rich man to enter Heaven than it was for the poor man to pass through the eye of a needle.

Having amassed the requisite money to sustain a pilgrimage, the first step of the pilgrim was to acquire the permission of the parish priest to undertake the journey, which would be given readily in return for a donation. For the duration of the journey, wealth was entrusted to the Crown or to the Church, and wives were given power to run their husbands' affairs in their absence. There was a fair universality of pilgrims' costume, which was functional and utilitarian. They wore a heavy coat and a wide-brimmed hat as protection against the sun and rain, and they carried a staff for support, with a water carrier attached, and a small satchel called a 'scrip'. The pilgrims also travelled in this utilitarian garb because it was recognisable, and they hoped it would afford them both protection and access to food and shelter. Some illustrations show medieval pilgrims wearing leather sandals and boots, while others – presumably the poorer and/or more penitent – went barefoot. Having arrived at their destination, however, the footsore traveller had some compensations. Footbaths were often available for washing bruised and dirty feet – there is one such at Iona. There the Benedictines had even constructed a wide, paved and drained 'Street of the Dead' around the main holy sites to ease sightseeing.

Many pilgrims wore badges (or 'sinacula') indicating the shrines and places they had visited, and the sale of these was a valuable source of income to the Church. James I gave pilgrims to Whithorn a safe conduct in 1427 – they were instructed to wear a certain badge on their outward journey, and another bought at Whithorn on their return. The nuns at North Berwick controlled the lucrative sale of St Andrew's badges for the journey to the shrine there. These souvenirs were regarded as having protective powers – unlike modern tourists' stickers and pennants.

The main centre of pilgrimage in medieval Scotland was St Andrews. The legend of St Andrew's relics (a tooth, three fingers, a kneecap and an arm bone) being brought to Scotland from his burial place in Greece was enough to establish the area where the cathedral now stands as a place of pilgrimage (there is a record of an Irish prince dying there while on pilgrimage in 967AD). A hospital maintained by Culdee monks existed to give shelter to the poorest pilgrims at this time; however, as it only catered for six, most pilgrims must have been able to afford private accommodation. It was in the period of the Wars of Independence, however, that the cult of St Andrew as Scotland's patron saint really flourished, and four years after Bannockburn, Robert the Bruce was present at the consecration of the hurriedly finished cathedral. All roads now led to St Andrews.

Along and around the pilgrimage routes an infrastructure to cater for the travellers sprang up: chapels, hospitals and inns were built, and later bridges over difficult rivers were constructed, which would have benefited general economic development. Roads, however, would have almost always been beaten out by the feet of men or horses, rather than deliberately built. As often as not these would have taken the form of ridgeways, avoiding the low, boggy and forested ground, and keeping high. The word 'road' was not used at this time, and clues to medieval pilgrims' and other roads are given by the appearance of the old Scots word 'gait' in the topographical record. In his book, *Pilgrimage in Medieval Scotland*, Peter Yeoman has outlined the main routes through the kingdom to St Andrews. Travellers from the north west left Perth and crossed a ferry at the confluence of the Tay and the Earn, passing the ancient route-marker of Macduff's Cross. From here an ancient 'green road' is still visible above Newburgh, which pilgrims followed to Lindores, where alms and shelter could be found at the abbey. The route then held to the higher ground north of Cupar, before crossing the Eden near Dairsie Castle, and continuing to St Andrews. Guardbridge became a gathering station for pilgrims from the west and north, before the last stage of the pilgrimage. Travellers from the north would have crossed the Tay around Tayport before joining up with those from the west at Guardbridge. Part of this latter route, being an ancient royal highway, was described in a charter of the time as being cobbled, but that must have been an unusual case for underfoot conditions.

The most important route to St Andrews was the one from the south, which crossed the Forth at Queen's Ferry. The ferry and the hostels on either side of the water which were 'to wait upon the pilgrims with great care', were endowed by Queen Margaret, according to her biographer Turgot, writing in 1093. At Inverkeithing pilgrims resided at the Franciscan friary, where the large guest range is still visible. From here the road went by a well-established route, mentioned as early as the 11th century as 'the public causeway which leads to Inverkeithing', and which boasted a bridge over the River Leven, before reaching the hospital at Scotlandwell where pilgrims were accommodated and cared for. The road then kept to the high ground north of the Leven valley, where a 14th century document records the existence of a 'Pilgrim Gait' to Ceres and then St Andrews.

Converging on St Andrews, the pilgrims would have seen the cathedral from a long way off, it being the largest building in medieval Scotland. Entering the city by one of the west gates, they passed rows of beggars and lepers as they approached the monastic precinct, along with stall-holders eager to sell their wares to the travellers. Entering the cathedral itself, they were shown round a building created to accommodate pilgrims and to hold the relics they came to see. Their visit completed, they were given a certificate as proof of their piety and remission from sin. If they were extremely lucky and had arrived on, for example, the feast of St Michael in the early 15th century, when the church was in sore need of money for rebuilding, they could purchase a plenary indulgence which granted remission from all sins and direct entry to Heaven. For believers, the days of footslogging, thirst and hunger, and the monies spent on subsistence, as well as their offerings to the Church and purchases of holy trinkets, must all have seemed worthwhile.

Although St Andrews was the main pilgrimage centre in medieval Scotland, it had its rivals, the chief of which was probably St Ninian's foundation of Candida Casa at Whithorn. Many of the pilgrims who visited Whithorn were from Ireland, and came in hide-covered coracles, but those from Scotland would have mainly walked – though (as elsewhere) the richest would have ridden on horseback, making up for their lack of hardship by the largesse of their contribution to the Church's wealth. Fifteenth century accounts describe the roads of Galloway as being thronged with pilgrims to Whithorn, and in 1504 King James IV met some 'puir folkis of Tayn passand to Whithorn'. There were various assembly points on the route to Whithorn including, ironically, a group of prehistoric standing stones at Laggangairn on the moors north of Glenluce Abbey, on which pilgrims have scratched crosses. Supporting the pilgrim infrastructure qualified for indulgences too, and the Countess of Douglas was granted one for rebuilding a bridge over the Bladnoch River 'where pilgrims to St Ninian assemble.' The mother of John Balliol, Devorguilla, endowed a timber bridge across the Nith at Dumfries in the 13th century to aid Whithorn pilgrims. The religious houses at Glenluce and Dundrennan, as well as inns, would have provided accommodation for the pilgrims.

Another Scottish king who made pilgrimage almost a way of life was James IV. He had much to atone for, coming to the throne in 1488 heavily implicated in the rebellion which had led to the death of his father. His first pilgrimages, to Whithorn in 1491 and to St Duthac's at Tain two years later, took place after his father's murder, and James probably felt he had squared that particular account with his conscience. Although doing penance for parricide by wearing a heavy iron belt, he continued to sin happily, indulging in many extra-marital dalliances, and even on occasion taking a mistress with him on pilgrimage, including 'Janet bare ars', as one Janet Kennedy was known. The Lord Treasurer's accounts of his pilgrimages give us a mixture of pleasure and piety, for as well as spending large sums on religious badges of one sort or another, James also lost heavily at cards on his journeys.

James' pilgrimages were renewed in 1507, and were concerned with his fears for the health of his ailing wife, Margaret Tudor, and his newborn and first legitimate son. In order to avoid the wrath of God descending on them for his own sins, James set out on an arduous pilgrimage to Whithorn, with a few followers. He undertook the whole journey on foot, and followed what was probably the standard pilgrims' route from Edinburgh to Dolphinton, Crawford, Durisdeer and Penpont, which he reached after five days, and where he had his shoes re-soled. (If the King's shoes wore out after 100 miles, medieval shoes must have been fairly frail productions.) Another three days took him to Dalry, Penninghame and Wigtown; a total of about 160 miles in eight days. Eagerly he carried on through the night to arrive at Whithorn in time for morning mass. His wife recovered, and went back with him to Whithorn the same year.

These journeys of the King were also opportunities to cement his reign by making offerings at various religious institutions, meeting local power brokers, and showing himself off as regally as possible to the masses en route. Similar political motivations lay behind his pilgrimages to Tain, which lay in an area where the power of the Lords of the Isles had recently been curbed – displaying the royal flag and venerating a local saint would do no harm, and James visited this far-flung pilgrimage outpost at least 18 times.

But possibly the good Lord was not mocked, for James' devotion to St Duthac did him little good. His last visit to the shrine at Tain was a month before the Battle of Flodden, in order to ask for the saint's protection. It was withheld, and James and almost 10,000 Scots died in a futile war against England, serving French interests. Within half a century, the abuses of indulgences and profiteering which had crept into pilgrimage were swept away, along with the institution itself, in the Reformation.

Suggested Walks

WALK 5

The Laggangairn Stones (OS 76 and 82)

From New Luce a minor road goes north-east to Balmurrie where it joins the Southern Upland Way heading northwards. This continues north across the Mulniegarroch or Purgatory Burn – the latter apparently named after a medieval lepers' colony hereabouts, whose members used the burn for washing. The route carries on through a plantation and in a clearing are the Laggangairn Stones, of which reputedly there used to be many more, before local pillaging reduced them to the present pair.

So far we are probably pretty much on the pilgrim's gait, but thereafter it is not really followable, though those wishing for more exercise can continue north and then east on the Southern Upland way to Darloskine Bridge, if pick-up transport can be arranged. On the way thence a side path leads to Linn's Tomb, the grave of a local Covenanter executed in the Killing Times of the 1680s, for here we are deep in their heartland.

From New Luce to Laggangairn: 6 miles, 3 hours; double time for the return trip.

To Darloskine Bridge from New Luce: 12 miles, 6 hours.

WALK 6

Clydesdale to Durisdeer. On the Trail of James IV (OS 78)

This is the only part of James IV's long route from Edinburgh to Whithorn that is not now totally covered by tarmac; it would also have been the hardest part of the journey. It followed the route of the old Roman Road from Clydesdale to Galloway, so as a historical walk it is a two for one offer. James' accounts of 1497 show an item 'to the wife of Durisdeer, where the King lodged, 14s'.

The route starts at Elvanfoot and between there and the Glenochar Burn the dedicated can follow the track of much of the old road to the west of the present one. Thereafter for four miles, until the Cleuch Burn, the former road is now the tarmacadamised A702. It is more pleasant, though not the exact route, to take the forestry track which starts at Watermeetings and goes south to Coom Rig, where it joins the Southern Upland Way before crossing the Potrail Water. Here another faintish part of the old road can be followed till it re-crosses both the A702 and the Potrail Water. The Romans and pilgrims did not take the current road's route through the Dalveen Pass, but struck over south between Well Hill and Durisdeer Hill before dropping down the Kirk Burn to Durisdeer. There is a well-preserved Antonine fortlet just above Durisdeer, whose old kirk is also worth visiting.

Elvanfoot to Durisdeer: 11 miles, 5–6 hours.

CHAPTER 4

Early Modern Walkers

TWO CONTRASTING WALKERS form the subject of this section. About one we know quite a lot, having the first-hand account of the journey he undertook. The personality and motives of the other lie shrouded in mystery, although he left behind a detailed relic of his journeys in map form.

Of the life of Timothy Pont little is known; more is known about his father, a leading figure in the Scottish Reformation who helped to draw up the Kirk's *Book of Discipline*. Timothy Pont was born in the early 1560s, and graduated from St Andrews University in 1583. He was a minister in Dunnet, Caithness, for a decade or so until about 1610, and probably died around four years afterwards, when he vanishes from records. We know little more about him. He travelled around Scotland from about 1583 until roughly 1596, and upon these journeys his map work was based. The motivation for his travels, however, is unclear.

Pont's work was known to others in his lifetime, but it was not published until 1654 in Amsterdam, in Blaeu's *Atlas* – a compendium of maps of the then-known world. One of those involved in the task was Robert Gordon of Straloch, in Aberdeenshire. Also a cartographer, Gordon had talked with Pont, and confirms in a letter that the map-maker's journeys were made on foot, but gives no clue as to his motive:

> He [Pont] travelled on foot through the whole of the Kingdom, as no one before him had done; he visited all the islands, occupied for the most part by inhabitants

hostile and uncivilised, and with a language different from our own; being often stripped, as he told me, by fierce robbers, and suffering not seldom, all the hardships of dangerous journeys, nevertheless at no time was he overcome by the difficulties, or disheartened.

The evidence from Pont's sketches, upon which the maps in the eventual *Atlas* were based, is indeed that he travelled through 'the whole of the Kingdom', and thus had a knowledge of the country surpassing that of anyone before him. Gordon was heavily responsible for the map of Aberdeenshire and Banffshire, but the vast bulk of the work was the result of Pont's labours, by hand and on foot. He had covered and mapped the whole of the Southern Uplands and Borders, and the Central Lowlands and Highlands of Scotland, all of which have detailed extant maps. There are fewer maps of the Western Highlands and Islands, but the evidence is that these were lost rather than not executed.

That any one person could, in the social and physical conditions of the late 16th century, have undertaken such journeys is impressive. That Pont could, in addition, have taken the time to map the areas he visited to a good standard is almost incredible. He recorded the human features of the countryside – habitations, churches and other significant buildings, especially fortifications. This suggests one possible motivation for his undertaking: that he was a spy. The fact that he also recorded natural resources (fishing, mineral deposits and suchlike) has led to another suggestion: that he was a prospector. However, Pont also recorded the physical features of the land, such as rivers, lochs and mountains. These latter are sometimes drawn in great detail, and were probably given as landmarks for the traveller. The illustration of Ben

Nevis, for example, in his map of the Lochaber area, depicts the mountain as it would be seen by a traveller crossing from Rannoch Moor to Fort William.

Pont probably followed the water-courses, which provided reasonably reliable means of communication. In addition, he would have had guides to take him across country. Without Gaelic himself, Pont gives place names in the Highlands, including mountains, in a form of Gaelic orthography. But there is other evidence that he must have had guides. A series of Pont's sketches show outlines of 'Ptalloch' (An Teallach) and other mountains, including those of Torridon such as 'Liachann' (Liathach), which can only be obtained from striking across country from Loch Maree. Comparing the maps to the terrain, there is little doubt that Pont crossed Loch Maree, traversed the mountains to where now lies Carnmore, and then crossed another range to come into Strath na Sealga, eventually reaching Little Loch Broom. In the map of the Strath, Pont inserts the notation for woodland, and adds that the area has 'excellent Hunting . . . where are deir [sic] to be found all the year long as in a mechtie Parck of nature.' Such a traverse from Loch Maree to Loch Broom is, even today, a very arduous undertaking, and in Pont's day it could only have been done with a guide.

Pont scribbled pieces of information on his maps. In western Sutherland, he informs us, there are 'black flies souking mens blood' and, even more worryingly, 'many Wolfs in this cuntry', compensated by 'good tak of herrings' and 'heir perle' at Loch Stack. At Loch 'Mulruy' (Maree) he tells us that there is a huge resource of timber, both of fir and oak, which is just waiting to be made into masts and planks. Pont was receptive to the splendour of the Highlands, describing the scenery around the loch as 'beautiful to look on', and Kintail as 'a fair and sweet countrey'. And as with other travellers at this period, the sheer abundance of wildlife never ceases to impress him. Of Strathnaver we are told that 'it is well stored with wood', and 'with fishes both from the sea and its own rivers. As also of dear, roe and dyvers kinds of wild beasts, especially here never lack wolves.' Much of the information which he scribbled on his sketch maps, or wrote in his various other accounts, was based on personal observation. Not so, however, the information that in Lewis there was a mountain where the deer had two tails, and a loch where the fish had four feet.

About his travels we know much, but about Pont himself we know almost nothing, though he was a man of intense curiosity, possibly a little gullible, and had an eye for natural beauty. In contrast, for our next pedestrian, John Taylor, we are provided with a very full character sketch, much of it from his own hand.

The Union of the Crowns in 1603 created some resentment against Scotland in England, as King James VI and I arrived in London with a determination to lay his hands on a share of England's wealth. The Union also created an increased curiosity about the northern country, and Jamie the Saxt was keen to encourage good reports about his native kingdom in his adoptive one. This gave an opportunity to persons keen to provide a spin-doctored account of Scotland. A quick-witted London bargee seized his chance – and in the process walked into areas where probably no Englishman had ventured before.

John Taylor was a sculler, or bargee, on the River Thames. He was a character, trying to sail the sea in a paper boat and playing other pranks. He was also a poet admired by King James, though of little real distinction. Participation in the organisation of an aquatic royal pageant in 1613 allowed him access to the Earl of Mar, who invited him to Scotland. This was an opportunity for an adventurous vacation, so Taylor – known as the Water Poet – jumped at the chance. However (partly as a publicity stunt, and partly as a wager) he vowed to undertake the journey on foot, and relying on Scottish generosity, without spending a penny: hence the title of his subsequent account, *The Pennyles* [sic] *Pilgrimage*. (Visitors today might attempt to meet the former stipulation, but I would advise against attempts to fulfil the latter.)

The year was 1618. Though Taylor undertook his pilgrimage on foot, he was accompanied by his 'man' on horseback. If Taylor is to be believed, he took no advantage of the horse, mentioning that while his man rode across the Esk and the Annan rivers on his first day's journey, he himself waded and was soaked to the skin. The first day was a marathon, and the duo travelled to 'Mophot' (Moffat) from Carlisle, a distance (according to the bargee) of 30 Scots or 40 English miles. Taylor comments 'that dayes journey [was] the weariest that I ever footed'. For even the fittest walker, such a distance would entail a minimum of 15 hours' walking, and one must have a sneaking suspicion that the sculler took advantage of the horse. At any rate he was exhausted by this over-exertion, and the next day he slowed down to 21 miles, and on the subsequent one 15, which brought him to Edinburgh. En route he had slept in primitive conditions, including an inn where pigeons shat on him from the rafters as he slept, but in 'Edenborough' things improved. Without contacts he approached a stranger in the street and explained his predicament, and was treated to a meal, drink and lodgings. He saw Edinburgh Castle and commented that all castles 'must give place to this unconquered castle, both for strength and scituation [sic]', while of the High Street he commented, with a hyperbole that would have warmed Jamie's heart, 'I observed the fairest and goodliest streete that even mine eyes beheld'.

Taylor crossed the River Forth by the ferry to Kinghorn in Fife, and then walked via Burntisland and Dunfermline to Stirling and 'Saint Johnstoun' (Perth). In Fife he had a contact in Sir George Bruce, a confidant of James VI, and a near neighbour of the Earl of Mar – who was not at home when Taylor visited Alloa Tower. Bruce had developed Scotland's greatest industrial undertaking at that time, in the form of his coal mines in Culross. The face was actually under the Forth, and a ventilation shaft built on a tidal island gave access to the workings, whence the coal was extracted through a mile-long tunnel. Taylor gained access to the face by sea and returned by the tunnel, and was amazed, saying he had not heard 'of any worke of man that might parallel with this unmatchable worke'. People like Bruce provided Taylor with hospitality, knowing James' affection for the Water Poet. The Earl of Mar had gone to his Highland estates near Braemar on a hunting holiday, and Taylor followed. He walked from Perth to Brechin – a distance of 32 miles – in a day, and from Brechin crossed the Mounth Road through Glen Esk to Deeside. Here he makes one of his surprisingly few comments about the state of the roads, noting that this section was 'uneven, stony and full of bogges', and that 'the way was rocky and not above a yard broad in some places'. Taylor stopped in 'Glaneske', where at 'an Irish house, the folkes not being able to speak scarce any English... I supped and went to bed...' only to have his sleep disturbed by 'Irish muskataes' feeding on his flesh.

The next day he travelled 'over an exceedingly high mountaine, called mount Skeen' (Mount Keen), and was engrossed in a 'Scottish miste' which caused him to 'moysten thorow all my clothes' and freeze, his teeth chattering, before arriving thankfully in the Braes o' Mar and joining up with his host on a vast hunting party in the Mar Forest. This lasted 12 days, and resulted in a huge slaughter of animals and birds, which amazed Taylor, who comments on the abundance of game in the area, including still extant wolves. He says the Highlanders presented a colourful picture in their 'Tartane' and plaids. On their footwear, he observes that the Highlanders wore 'shoes with but one sole apiece', which suggests that Taylor's own footwear was strengthened with layers of soles. He was also impressed by the forest cover. To an England experiencing a timber-shortage, the sculler remarks:

> For I dare affirme [the Earl of Marre] hath as many firre-trees growing there as would serve for masts (from this time till the end of the worlde) for all the shippes, carackes, hoyes, galleyes, boates, drumbles, barkes and water-crafts that are now, or can be in the world these fourty yeeres.

From the Braes o' Mar, Taylor travelled to Speyside, or 'Bagenoch'. He does not give the route, but it was probably through Glen Feshie, a lower and easier route than the Lairig Ghru, and one which directly reaches Badenoch on Upper Speyside. Thereafter he walked to Elgin, and back to 'Breekin' by the 'Carney Mount' (Cairn o' Mounth), the pass between Banchory and Brechin, and a much lower one than the Glen Esk Road. At Brechin he had an adventure when a deaf and dumb Scottish serving wench tried to force her attentions on him, and he was obliged to barricade his door against her. Obviously he was saving his energies for his final walk back to Edinburgh, where he arrived after tramping continuously for about a month and a half. He rode from there back to London, where his memoir was published to great acclaim. Taylor ends with an outburst of praise to Scotland, pointing out that despite the praise he has lavished on the country:

> I vow to God, I have done Scotland wrong,
> And, justly, 'gainst me it may bring an action
> I have not given't the right which doth belong
> For which I am halfe guilty of detraction...

This must have brought a rare smile to the greetin' face of the 'Wisest Fool in Christendom'.

Suggested Walks

WALK 7

Loch Maree to Dundonnell (OS 19)

From the evidence of his maps, it is clear that Timothy Pont travelled this way in the 1590s. James Hogg, the Ettrick Shepherd, followed in 1803, and found the route difficult. It still is so, and should only be attempted by strong, experienced and well-equipped walkers. In particular there can be some dangerous, at times impossible, river crossings.

The route is best done from the Loch Maree end. It is possible to execute the walk using public transport, as regular buses serve both Poolewe and Dundonnell from Inverness.

From Poolewe the route goes along the north side of the River Ewe to Kernsary, and then up the Allt na Creige. This path has recently been upgraded all the way to Carnmore bothy, and modern users will never know its previous horrors.

A causeway leads to Carnmore between the Dubh and Fionn lochs. Carnmore is a magnificent setting but a cheerless doss and most will continue over the col to Gleann na Muice Beag amidst ever more fabulous scenery to the Abhainn Strath na Sealga, where An Teallach looms to the north. Pont called this area 'a mechtie parck of nature' and it is indeed. The crossing of the river here calls for extreme care. It can be a walk over a shallow gravel bed, or the entire glen can become a huge, raging loch. Across the river is the wonderful Shenavall bothy, where good accommodation can be had, or it is possible to complete a long hard day by ascending another 400 m over the shoulder of An Teallach and down the sylvan Gleann Chaorachainn to Corrie Hallie and the end of a day of days.

Poolewe to Corrie Hallie: 23 miles (another 3 miles to the Dundonnell Hotel), 12–15 hours. Or Poolewe to Shenavall: 18 miles, 9–10 hours, and overnight.

WALK 8

Glen Esk to Deeside (OS 44)

About a decade after Pont did the above walk, Taylor the Water Poet completed the easier one described here. The Mounth Road as it became known, was later to become a drove road, a seasonal reapers' route and latterly a whisky smugglers' road.

You should be dropped at the road end about a mile east of Loch Lee and make your way up Glen Mark past a well commemorating Queen Victoria's 1861 pony crossing of this route, and begin ascending Mount Keen. The original Mounth Road passes the shoulder of the mountain on the west, but it is possible to combine the walk with an ascent of this, the most easterly Munro in Scotland, before descending into Glen Tanar. At Etnach is an old drovers' stance where there was once an inn, and further downriver lies the Half Way Hut, which offers a refreshment shelter in poor weather. The route ends in the pleasant wood- and river-scape around Glen Tanar house, beyond which it is possible to arrange a pick-up point.

Glen Esk to Glen Tanar: 16 miles, 7–8 hours.

CHAPTER 5

Jacobites and Hanoverians

THE MEN ASSEMBLED at Glenfinnan on 19 August 1745 to proclaim a Stewart restoration had not walked far. They had come by the glens of Lochaber; many, like the Camerons, marching only a few miles from their villages. Eight months later, fugitive, they sought their homes once more, and those who had stayed with Charles Edward Stewart since Glenfinnan had walked over 1,000 miles by the time of the defeat at Culloden.

In the middle of the 18th century, the Highlands, or rather the Central Highlands, were favoured in Scotland in having a decent system of roads, the work of General Wade. After the 1719 Rebellion, Wade was brought to Scotland and found the Highlands far from pacified. He immediately spent £10,000 on repairing forts, but realised the key to pacification lay in communications. Highland terrain was 'habitual to the natives, but very difficultly supported by the Regular Troops... for want of Roads and Bridges', and from 1724–40 he constructed 250 miles of roads and 40 bridges. (His successor, General Caulfeild, did better, with nearly 1,000 miles of road, mainly constructed post-pacification.)

Those who made the roads walked. The artist Paul Sandby did illustrations showing the surveying work which was done by an officer and six soldiers on foot, carrying a theodolite and measuring chains. The actual road building was done in the months of April to October and was carried out by the soldiers themselves, who were paid double time for the work. There were 500 men on each road, working in groups of 100 at stations 10 miles apart, to which they walked and where they lived in huts or under canvas. With pick-axes, crowbars and shovels they cleared the way for the laying of a base of boulders, topped with smaller stones and gravel, to a general width of 16 feet or so, which would allow vehicles to pass or to turn. These roads were meant to facilitate the movement of Hanoverian troops, but they allowed the Jacobite army in 1745 to leave the Highlands quicker than it might otherwise have done. The roads, however, came into their own after Culloden, allowing a swift pacification of the Highlands which would have been inconceivable after the 1715 Rebellion.

Attempts were made to mould the Jacobite forces into a regular army, but these had limitations. The men were poorly armed and trained. Desertion was rife, especially among the many who had been coerced into rebellion, and the army held together partly because discipline was only moderately enforced – on occasion Highland troops refused to dig trenches because manual labour was beneath them! Pay became increasingly irregular as the campaign wore on, and many troops were in serious arrears by the time of Culloden. Another problem was that although an army marches on its stomach, it also marches on its feet, and in the wherewithal for this the Jacobites were deficient. And the Jacobites did walk – out of 5,000 men, less than 400 possessed horses.

Most Highlanders at this time would have gone barefoot for normal occasions, but on longer journeys wore brogues or shoes. The Jacobites moved quickly from Glenfinnan to the Corrieyairack Pass, and occupied its heights before General Cope. After the latter had fled towards Inverness, the way south to Edinburgh on the fine military road was open. For this march south the rebel band wore footwear –

walking on a surfaced road is nigh impossible barefoot. By the time the Jacobite army occupied Edinburgh, the footwear (and possibly the feet) of their recruits would have been in a poor state. It is no surprise that Charles ordered the city fathers to deliver 6,000 pairs of shoes to his army the day after he took Edinburgh. Once the army of Cope had been defeated at Prestonpans, the dead were stripped of their footwear, and many a wounded man was dirked for his boots as much as for his weapon. The same was true at the Battle of Falkirk in early 1746.

The demand for footwear is a constant aspect of the Jacobite advance and retreat which has attracted little notice from historians. At Preston on the march south, 'several thousands' of pairs of shoes were delivered to the Jacobites, and on the army's retreat the citizens of Dumfries paid for their anti-Jacobite sympathies by delivering 1,000 pairs of shoes to them from their soutars. Glasgow, moreover, was fiercely Hanoverian and some Jacobites wanted to torch the place, but this punishment was commuted to the delivery of Glaswegian supplies, including 6,000 pairs of shoes. The Jacobite strength varied from 2,000 to 9,000 men at various times under arms, probably averaging 5,000. Total requisitions of shoes appear to have been about 20,000, and assuming the men arrived to enlist with a pair, that means each man used approximately five pairs on the campaign, which covered about 1,000 miles. Shoes requisitioned would most probably have been civilian items from urban soutars. Roads were rough, and a single pair appears to have worn out in about 200 miles. Much of the time the Jacobites must have been footsore to a debilitating extent.

If they had footwear of decent quality, and *if* it fitted, the rebels had other problems. The Jacobite soldier did not travel especially light. He carried his dirk, a pistol and a broadsword if he had them, his musket (2,000 were taken after Culloden, and only 200 broadswords) and ammunition, as well as what personal kit he possessed, such as a blanket. Some carried their own water canteens, and all carried their day's ration of oatmeal in a sack (or 'pock'). Their clothing would have been heavy, especially when wet. That the Highlanders were tough is clear. Many made a virtue of their 'manliness', and Walter Scott gives the tale of a father who kicked away a son's pillow made of snow, accusing him of effeminacy. They preferred to sleep outdoors in all weathers, and could only with difficulty be persuaded to occupy Cope's abandoned tents after Prestonpans. But the Highlander was not superhuman, and possibly not as tough as he himself, or his Hanoverian opponents (or indeed subsequent historians) thought.

Contemporaries inspired by terror, and historians inspired by those contemporary accounts, have generally argued that the Jacobite army was faster than their Hanoverian opponents, who had great difficulty catching them as they could not match the speed in advance – or retreat – of their enemies. This view conceals the Jacobites' Achilles heel, to use a pedestrian metaphor. Charles' army advanced south from the Corrieyairack, managing Dalwhinnie to Dalnacardoch in a day, and Blair Atholl in another day; they also did Dunkeld to Perth in a day. All of these were solid advances, accounting for 20 miles per diem. In England they achieved similar feats, reaching Kendal two days after leaving Carlisle, and covering the ground from Manchester to Derby in three and a half days; again 15–20 miles a day on average. Evacuating Glasgow on their retreat on 3 January, the Jacobites pitched camp near Stirling, a distance of 23 miles away; a remarkable feat.

What these impressive figures conceal is the price at which they were bought. Charles halted for two days at Blair Atholl, three at Kendal, and for similar lengths of time at other stages on his journey. These halts were partly to gain recruits and to amass supplies, but mainly they were because the army was exhausted. All armies need to rest, but some, and the Jacobite army was one, need to rest more than others. The Jacobites were physically incapable of maintaining the pace set over longer periods. Lord George Murray, when discussing the attempted night march to attack Cumberland's camp prior to Culloden, mentions that 'the Highlanders had often marched more than two miles an hour', feeling that they would reach the camp before dawn and have the advantage of surprise. Two miles an hour is not a brilliant feat at the best of times, emphasising that the Highlanders' long distance bursts were accomplished not so much by speed as by long marching periods.

Nairn, and Cumberland's camp, was a little over 10 miles away, and leaving at about 8pm, the Highlanders were expected to arrive by 2am. The men had not been fed and had been out all day in bad weather. In the dark they got lost, were slowed by dykes, and at dawn were not even at the camp. These same men repeated the march back to Culloden where many fell into an exhausted sleep, only to be woken by Cumberland's guns; they had still not eaten. Hypothermia and hypoglycaemia probably account as much for Jacobite indecision on the Drumossie Moor, as do poor and divided leadership. The pain of hunger, cold, aching limbs and lacerated feet must have made many rebels indifferent as to whether they lived or died. The Jacobites' supplies were fairly regular, and not simply based on marauding, but they were not as regular as their rivals', and became increasingly irregular as their campaign wore on.

One historian's description of the 'well-fed' Hanoverian army facing the 'starving Highland peasants' at Culloden cannot be wide of the mark.

What of the Hanoverian opposition? Despite traditional hostility in Britain to a standing army, the British army in 1745 was reasonably well-equipped and armed and, importantly, was comfortably provisioned in comparison to its enemies. Certainly Cumberland's army was well fed, with brick ovens being built every night to bake bread, and little shortage of food for the troops. Additionally, their footwear would have been either military boots, which gave support to the foot and protection to the leg, or shoes and gaiters, which made the footwear more effective and durable. They were under cover at night, the men usually in tents, and the officers billeted in local houses.

This provisioning is regarded by some as being a disadvantage when dealing with an army such as the Jacobites. It is argued that the supply-trains which accompanied the Hanoverian army – though much of these supplies went on the ships of the British navy – slowed down Cumberland and the others and gave the Jacobites a tactical advantage. But whatever advantage the Jacobites had, speed was not one of them. Cope marched from Stirling to Dalwhinnie in six days, while by a slightly different route south the Jacobites arrived at Perth from Dalwhinnie in six days also – a shorter distance than Cope had travelled in the same time.

When the Jacobites turned at Derby and began to retreat, Cumberland's army was two days' march away from the rebels. On the retreat, by the time the Jacobites reached the Lake District, Cumberland was snapping at their heels, and at Clifton the Jacobite rearguard encountered and repulsed the Hanoverian advanced guard. Within 150 miles, Cumberland had gained on the Jacobites. The evidence is that while the Jacobites could outpace their opponents over a couple of days, Cumberland's better equipped and clothed troops had more stamina, and could outdo the enemy over a longer period. At Stafford on 4 December 1745, after a forced march, Cumberland halted his troops for a rest of only one day, giving the reason that:

> troops that had scarcely halted in these seven days, and had been without victuals for 24 hours, and had been exposed to one of the coldest nights I ever felt without any shelter, were not able to march without a halt.

There is no record in 1745 of a similar feat of endurance by the Jacobite army. The Hanoverians' ability to undertake such sustained walking over a longer period counter-balanced any advantage that the Jacobites had with their possibly swifter immediate movements.

The slowness of Cumberland's advance through Scotland to Aberdeen, where he stayed with his army for six weeks, had little to do with the drag of baggage and camp followers. He felt that time would work its attrition on Jacobite numbers, and was right. He wanted to allow the hospitalised to recover, as well as for the River Spey – whose crossing he expected to be contested – to fall after the spring floods, and for the grass to begin growing for his horses. He also used the time to train his men in methods of combating the Highland charge.

Cumberland was a competent rather than a brilliant general, but he was effective at counter-insurgency warfare. His men slept in their uniforms and marched with bayonets fixed, instantly ready for combat. When he moved forward to Culloden, his troops' speed matched anything achieved by the Jacobites. Cumberland walked his men at an average of about 15 miles a day. He marched from Aberdeen to Nairn in six days, a distance of about 90 miles in total, including one forced march of 20 miles. The Jacobites' best continuous march was probably that from Edinburgh to Carlisle, achieved from 3 to 9 November 1745 – about 85 miles in seven days. The per diem calculations just do not support the idea of the Jacobites having the advantage of speed over their enemies.

Even in hit-and-run operations, the British army was (latterly) almost a match for the Jacobites. In early 1746, 300 foot soldiers and 100 dragoons set out from Aberdeen to attack Corgarff Castle, where rebels were massing. After 'two nights in the open fields [three days' travel]... over mountains and Moors, almost impassable at any time of year, but much more so when covered with snow', they arrived at the castle to find the fire on and a cat at the hearth, but the rebels gone. From Aberdeen to Corgarff is more than 50 miles, so the men had travelled at over 16 miles a day in mid-winter, with three-quarters of their complement on foot. They returned in a similar time, with their powder and their feet (in well-made boots) dry.

After the Battle of Culloden on 16 April 1746, the defeated fled on foot – only to be pursued, largely on foot, by their victors. But the most amazing tramping achievement of this period was that of Charles Stewart himself. For five months he eluded his pursuers, almost entirely on foot. He was ill-clad and certainly ill-shod, and he often went without food and spent many nights in the open, experiencing in a heightened form the hardships many of his soldiers had undergone. He covered several hundred miles in this time, over terrain much worse than that which his army had passed through. This period led to his enshrinement as a hero, and helped to erase memories of a man who had led thousands to an ill-deserved fate.

The authorities expected further risings after Culloden, and defences like Fort George were built. Caulfeild's roads were also pushed through the glens. The Hanoverians, who liked to see themselves as the legatees of the Romans, had achieved the pacification of the Caledonian tribes, a task which had eluded their predecessors.

Suggested Walks

WALK 9

The Great Glen to Speyside by the Corrieyairack Pass (OS 34)

This was a route between the above areas, long before General Wade engineered it in 1731. It almost saw a battle in 1745 as the Jacobite army advanced to the head of the pass from Glenfinnan in the west, and General Cope's troops reached the foot of the pass from the east before retreating to Inverness without offering combat. Since the Jacobites covered the whole route, to their footsteps go the honour of our following.

Just south of Fort Augustus the A82 meets the B862. The route begins a little to the north of the junction on the B road. It takes the higher ground to the south of Glen Tarff to Blackburn before crossing the Allt Lagan a' Bhainne, where the Redcoats camped while building the road. Then it climbs through wildening country till it reaches the summit of the pass at 775 m. Thence zig zags descend steeply into Corrie Yairack, though these carefully engineered bends have been damaged, as have other aspects of this road, by electricity supply vehicles for the pylons crossing the path, as well as by four wheel drive vehicles which are able to use this road, as it was sadly never declassified. A real atrocity committed upon a scheduled Ancient Monument.

The road then descends to Melgarve where there is an extant Wade bridge, and where there was once an inn and a drovers' stance; now there is an open bothy where you can shelter overnight. The tarred road begins a little east of Melgarve, but it is well to continue three miles further down to the Spey to Garva Bridge where a wonderful double arched Wade bridge crosses the Spey. Just beyond, at Garvamore, is one of the Hanoverians' military outposts established after the '45. I always think a less incompetent general than Cope could have stopped Charlie at Garva Bridge. It is a good place for you to stop too, and await your lift.

Fort Augustus to Garvamore: 19 miles, 10 hours.

WALK 10

Prince Charlie's Cave and Sgurr nan Conbhairean (os 34)

The forensic delineation of the wanderings of Bonnie Prince Charlie after Culloden is not a totally exact science, and there are more caves bearing his name than he could possibly have slept in during his flight. However, one cave which he definitely used can be visited, and combined, if wished, with the ascent of a mountain upon whose summit he spent at least one night.

A mile east of where the A887 meets the A87 lies Ceannacroc Lodge. From there a very stony Land Rover track heads up the River Dho until the latter splits. Here take the Allt Coire Mheadhoin (no path) until its head where, amongst a jumble of massive and unmissable boulders, is

Charlie's Cave. This has a sandy floor and a burn running through it, and inside is an unmistakable bed recess, which, when I slept there, was filled with turf and heather. On the outside wall is a plaque, in Gaelic, commemorating the Pretender's residence.

An easy walk takes you up grassy slopes to the summit of Sail Chaorainn, and turning south you soon ascend Sgurr nan Conbhairean, as did the Prince himself. Descending the Glas Bealach you pick up a path along the Allt Coire Sgreumh which leads back to the River Dho.

To Charlie's Cave: 8 miles, 4 hours.

To the summit of Conbhairean as well: 10 miles, 6 hours.

CHAPTER 6

The English Tourists

THE PACIFICATION OF THE HIGHLANDS was a necessary pre-condition to the opening of the region to travellers. The development of Romanticism, with its positive attitude to wild scenery and the less civilised aspects of the human condition, transformed Caledonia into a living museum of the picturesque, and there was an increase in visitor numbers. The Napoleonic Wars closed the continent to English travellers for long periods. The common war against France cemented the identity of Scotland as North Britain, and it became an acceptable location for an alternative to the Grand Tour – without the sunshine. Some of the 'tourists', as they were already known, came seeking artistic inspiration. In this section we meet a painter, George Fennel Robson, who found exactly what he wanted, and a poet, John Keats, who did not.

The critic Ruskin, whose writings did much to mould appreciation of the mountain landscape, thought highly of Robson's works and said, 'They are serious and quiet in the highest degree, [and] certain qualities of atmosphere and texture in them have never been equalled.' Robson was born in Durham in 1788, at the beginning of the Romantic enthusiasm. He became the President of the Old Watercolours Society in 1819, in recognition of his achievement in mountain painting. He painted in Snowdonia, and made tours of the Scottish Highlands, getting as far as Loch Coruisk in Skye.

Robson delved deep into the mountains on foot. He was inspired by the vogue for Walter Scott and, dressing himself in a tartan plaid and hose, set off with the Wizard of Abbotsford's works about his person. His equipment was carried on a pony, but he walked, and covered many miles sketching. In 1814 appeared his 'Scenery of the Grampian Mountains', produced for a large number of subscribers. These were pen and ink drawings, but they were so successful that an aquatint edition was produced five years later. In the days before photography, Robson's collection of 40 outlines of the mountains from the Trossachs to the Braes of Mar (with a bonus one of Ben Nevis) would in all probability have been, for most of its purchasers, their first impression of what the Highlands looked like.

Though romantically dramatised, the peaks in Robson's folio are instantly recognisable, due to their excellent draughtsman-like execution. These were artworks born of love and Robson expresses great delight and awe in the scenery. He climbed several peaks, including Braeriach in the Cairngorms, saying:

> neither difficulty nor danger should deter the tourist, who has reached the foot of Braeriach, from visiting the summit... let him approach, with cautious steps, the brink of the precipice... In a situation so exalted, admiration is raised to enthusiasm.

Robson also appears to have ascended and traversed Beinn a' Bhuird. He was a strong walker, as can be seen from following his progress through the Grampian mountains. We do not, however, know how long this odyssey took the painter; he probably stopped frequently, and speed would not have been of the essence.

Robson started his tour at Stirling, from which he said the tourist 'will find a good road' to Aberfoyle, and then 'a rough road across the mountains to the Trosachs [sic]'. He then made a series of side trips, including one to Loch Lomond and Arrochar to draw Ben Lomond, which he ascended, describing the view from its summit. He headed north by Glen Ogle to Killin, sketching Ben Vorlich en route, and made a side trip to Tyndrum. Robson moved along the south side of Loch Tay, and drew Ben More and later Schiehallion, and then went by Tummel to Dunkeld, before continuing northwards through Killiecrankie, where he composed a prospect of the Beinn a' Ghlo massif. So far he had been almost entirely on the military roads built in the previous century, but now things were to change.

Robson's map showed a road from Blair Atholl to Deeside, but he found it did not exist. As he moved up Glen Tilt, he noted 'the scenery becomes gradually more rude and dreary, and the road soon inaccessible to carriages'. He plodded on and came to the ford at the Poll Tarf (the Falls of Tarf), where he was astounded by:

> a scene worthy of the pencil of Salvator... nowhere... will be found to possess a more picturesque combination of wild and characteristic beauty than this... it is in every respect faultless.

Despite the reference to Salvator Rosa, the Italian mountain artist, and the perfection of the Tarf, Robson did not draw it. He probably wanted to get over the 'bleak and gloomy desert' ahead and into Aberdeenshire by nightfall.

On Deeside he continued, walking to and drawing the great peaks of Ben Macdhui (Macdui) and Braeriach, as well as visiting the Shelter Stone. Robson's comments on the roads, or rather 'paths', are unvarying. To Loch Avon, he says, 'the path is difficult', and while heading for the Chest of Dee 'the difficulties of the path increase'. Although Robson penetrated the Lairig Ghru as far as Braeriach and ascended the mountain, what he saw there discouraged a complete traverse of the pass. He commented on the lairig that 'the way is long and difficult, and no place of shelter or refreshment occurs in this direction'. Instead, he went to Speyside 'by the great road which runs between the eastern and western coasts of Scotland' – this was probably the Lecht military road.

As well as enjoying the scenery of the Grampians, Robson enjoyed meeting the inhabitants, despite the language barrier. In Glen Lyon the people ran out of their shielings and dragged the painter in for feeding. 'Their habitations are rude and comfortless huts, and their best food is milk, oatmeal and potatoes... yet these poor people are given to hospitality.' In Braemar he finds another quality to admire:

> The cottages in this district seem destined for the abode of wretchedness... the floor is naked earth, smoke and darkness prevail within... [yet t]he inhabitants of these miserable hovels are in general much better informed, and seem endowed with quicker capacities, than the peasantry of England.

Robson also assured any timid souls that 'the influence of civilisation has at length subdued the ferocity of the Highlander, who is now distinguished for civility and intelligence'. But not everyone who visited Scotland with romantic notions came away as pleased as Robson. For the poet John Keats, the country was, literally, a fatal disappointment.

Of the several English poets – including William Wordsworth – to visit Scotland at this period, Keats' account of his travels in his letters home is the most interesting. In

1818, at the age of 22, he set out north with his companion Charles Brown, with the intention of undertaking a 1,000 mile walk through Scotland (with a side-visit to Ireland). Unfortunately circumstances prevented him achieving his aim – which was to get as far as John o' Groats. A further aim was to seek artistic inspiration – to ascend 'the Ben Lomonds of his poetic imagination', as he put it. This aim was rather underachieved also, as the poetry he produced on the tour was rather, well, pedestrian, and he did not manage to ascend the real Ben Lomond either.

As a prelude to his Scottish walking, Keats set out from Lancaster to walk through the Lake District. He and Brown had oilskin capes (fortuitous, as they were to encounter much bad weather), knapsacks of toiletries and writing materials, and Keats carried volumes of Dante and Milton. Keats also mentions that they had maps with them, and that he had read fairly widely of previous travellers' accounts of Scotland.

The duo walked the 114 miles from Lancaster to Carlisle according to an unwise schedule, which they followed throughout their trip. This was to walk several miles before breakfast every day, stopping at mealtimes to read and write letters. Such a method led to a gradual erosion of bodily strength. Keats and Smith failed to climb Helvellyn, because of mist, but did ascend Skiddaw, before riding in a coach from Carlisle to Dumfries as they had heard there was nothing of interest on that section of their route.

Keats visited Burns' Mausoleum in Dumfries, but commented that it was 'not very much to my taste'. Then their walking tour started in earnest and they headed for Kirkcudbright, where Keats arrived 'tired after my day's walking and ready to tumble into bed' and also 'a little tired in the thighs and a little blistered'. He noted that the women they encountered walked barefoot, carrying their shoes and stockings. Thoughts of Meg Merrilies entertained him en route, but at Creetown he complained that 'the children jabber away as if in a foreign language', echoing most English travellers' distaste for the sound of Scots.

Keats' and Brown's method of walking without breakfast and covering long tracts of country ('Yesterday we came 27 miles from Stranraer', Keats wrote at Ballantrae) gave them a huge appetite. The poet wrote, rather unpoetically, 'I get so hungry I can eat a Bull's head as easily as I used to do Bull's eyes'. But the fare they were provided with in Scotland gave constant cause for complaint. At Newton Stewart the poet wrote, 'We dined yesterday on dirty bacon, dirtier eggs and dirtiest potatoes with a slice of salmon'.

Despite his dislike of the Scots language, Keats was an admirer of Burns' poetry, and this route was deliberately chosen in order to visit the place of Rab's birth outside Ayr. Keats 'stood some time on the Brig over which Tam o' Shanter fled', before visiting Kirk Alloway and Burns' cottage itself. Keats confessed himself to be underwhelmed, and took a dram and wrote a poem, more or less because he felt obliged to. Although Keats wrote that 'we bear the fatigue very well, 20 miles a day in general', one suspects that tiredness and undernourishment were dulling his poetic responses.

After passing through Glasgow, the pair arrived at Loch Lomond. Though Keats drew a picture of the loch and mountain, he abandoned any idea of climbing it, and they pressed on. He wrote, 'We got up at 4 this morning and have walked to breakfast 15 miles through two tremendous glens – so we were cheated into five more miles to breakfast.' They had expected the 'Rest and be Thankful' on the road from Loch Lomond to Inveraray to be an inn, but 'horror and starvation', as Brown put it, 'Rest and be Thankful was not an Inn, but a stone seat' (actually the 'seat' was a memorial to the building of the military road in 1768). The strain was beginning to tell. Keats remarks that Brown's feet were so blistered he was 'scarcely able to walk' as they went from Inveraray to Ford along Loch Awe, adding that his friend was 'knock'd up from new shoes'. So far the companions had been walking largely on the military roads, which would have been very severe on their feet.

Keats mentions other hardships. At Inveraray his meal was spoiled by a piper: 'Nothing could stifle the horrors of a solo on the Bag-pipe – I thought the Beast would never be done.' Not that the food found his favour either – generally they lived on eggs and oatcakes in the Highlands and expressed a deep longing for white bread. Leaving Inveraray the following day, alongside Loch Awe the pair hit rock bottom: 'We had eaten nothing but eggs all day – about 10 a piece, and they had become sickening.' Their misery was compounded when on a subsequent day they walked from Kilmelfort to Oban, 15 miles, in the pouring rain. Hardly conditions to inspire the muses!

Iona and Staffa were on their itinerary, and they crossed to the island of Mull. Through Glen More they were off the hard roads, but it was little consolation. Keats wrote of the track through the glen as 'the most dreary you can think of, over bog and rock and river with our Breeches tucked up and our stockings in hand'. On the island they were thoroughly soaked one day, and could find only a shepherd's hut for accommodation. Keats wrote: 'The family speak not a word but gaelic and we have not yet seen their faces for the smoke which finds its way out at the door.' Lying on an earthen floor in damp clothes, Keats – already weakened by exertion –

caught a severe chill and cold. At Oban, Brown commented that Keats' 'inflammation of the throat, occasioned by rainy days, fatigue and privation' was worsening.

A foolish decision followed – foiled by Ben Lomond, they decided to climb Ben Nevis, a massive strain on Keats' weakened system. Despite successfully ascending the summit, the poet again seemed under-inspired by the experience, and wrote one of his weaker poems to commemorate the event:

All my eye doth meet
Is mist and Crag – not only on this height
But in the world of thought and mental might...

Keats had earlier on the tour observed that, 'The first Mountains I saw weighed very solemnly on me. The effect is wearing away.' Pointing out that Ben Nevis is the highest mountain in Great Britain he adds, 'On that account I will never ascend another in this empire.'

From Fort William, the Wade road to Inverness was followed, and at the Highland capital the decision was taken, on doctor's advice, to head homewards. At Inverness on 7 August, Brown wrote, 'I have stumped away on my toes 642 miles.' Given that they had been travelling for 45 days, this makes an average of just under 15 miles a day; well below Keats' claimed 20 miles, and the evidence is that he and Brown simply could not maintain their early pace, which had included days of almost 30 miles. They took their final stroll to Dingwall, and sailed to London from Cromarty.

Keats never fully recovered from his ordeal, and was dead of tuberculosis at the age of 25.

Suggested Walks

WALK 11

Atholl to Deeside via the Falls of Tarf (OS 43)

This is one of the great passes of the Grampian Mountains, and was the occasion of a famous right of way battle in the 1840s, after the Duke of Atholl unsuccesfully tried to close it. Fennel Robson did the route with a pony carrying his artists' and other materials in one day; it is a long day.

Train or bus to Blair Atholl is the convenient way to start this walk, as you end far from the point of departure. By the Bridge of Tilt, then the route takes you along the west bank of the eponymous river to Gilbert's Bridge by fine wooded scenery. At Forest Lodge a keeper's house is passed, the one and only habitation along this route. The scene becomes wilder until you reach the Falls of Tarf, a spot Robson said was 'worthy of (Salvator) Rosa', a painter whose landscapes he admired. Robson forded the Poll Tarf, as did Victoria in 1861, but there is now a bridge. The increasingly narrow glen breasts the top of the pass just east of Loch Tilt, and then descends towards Deeside, passing the ruins of Bynack Lodge and Ruigh nan Clach before reaching White Bridge. Those who have carried a tent may care to camp hereabouts.

From White Bridge it is an easy and pleasant riverside walk to the Linn o' Dee, passing several ruined clachans where examples of lazybeds and limekilns can be spotted. At the Linn o' Dee the public road starts, but it is another 6 miles to Braemar and bus services to Aberdeen.

Blair Atholl to Linn o' Dee: 22 miles 11 hours; to Braemar: 28 miles, 14 hours.

WALK 12

Ben Nevis by the Tourist Route (OS 41)

Keats would have probably walked from Fort William along the east side of the River Nevis to Achintee House and then carried on up the now so-called Tourist Path. This road was actually constructed to take provisions to the Observatory which was established on the summit of the mountain in the later 19th century, and which was supplied by packmen walking daily there with laden ponies. At Lochan Meall an t-Suidhe was the Half Way House of the weathermen, where they took additional observations. Thereafter the track zig zags easily but monotonously to the summit, though in bad weather it is possible to lose the way near the plateau. The summit itself carries the ruins of the Observatory and also of a hotel which was briefly established there in the years before World War I. See *Twenty Years on Ben Nevis*, W.T. Kilgour (1905). Descend by the outward route.

Fort William to the summit of Ben Nevis: 8 miles, 5 hours.

Can be shortened by starting from the Youth Hostel in Glen Nevis, 5+ miles, 3–4 hours.

CHAPTER 7

Reivers and Drovers

PIRACY, IT HAS BEEN SAID, is the first stage of commerce. In relation to Scotland's cattle trade, illegal reiving was the first stage of legitimate droving. There was some limited trade in the beasts before the 16th century, and the right existed of spending the night on common land with cattle on the move. But the most usual early motive for the movement of cattle was theft. In 1554 English raiders drove 10,386 cattle south of the border, and all over Scotland itself the practice of stealing was endemic. Perpetrators of cattle theft were seldom caught and forced to face the rigours of the law.

In the Borders, the placing by the lady of the house of a bull's head on a platter was a signal that the larder was bare and it was time to go raiding. Border ballads tell of these raids, and 'Otterburn' was as much about thieving as a battle against the Auld Enemy. Interestingly, that ballad describes the Scots leader Douglas as 'riding to England to catch a prey' and notes 'The Jardines wouldna wi him ride/And they rue it tae this day'. Given the fact that the English knew the Borders as well as the Scots, and were well mounted themselves, it would indeed have been a foolhardy man who went a-thieving there on foot.

In the Highlands, it was different. The MacFarlans and MacGregors on Loch Lomondside would descend on foot at night to the lowlands, and be back in their mountain fastness immune from pursuit by early light. Those who tried to follow could meet an awful fate, as did the Colquhouns at Glen

Fruin when they chased raiding MacGregors in 1603 and lost 80 men in battle. In the reiving between clans, great distances were covered on foot. In 1644 a band of Campbells from Argyll despoiled the Angus Glens, only to be pursued and caught and forced to fight near the Cairnwell Pass, where several of the raiders fell. These, and the men of Glengarry who drove 2,700 cattle out of Glenisla and Glenshee in 1602, were undoubtedly learning an apprenticeship in cattle droving skills which their descendants would later put to good use.

Many of the drovers must have been sons or grandsons of bandits. (For a while this role-reversal could itself also be reversed. Rob Roy started as a drover, but by ill-luck was driven to banditry.) The beginnings of an organised internal/external trade in live beasts on any scale dates from the 16th century, when tolls on live cattle began to appear on bridges, for example at Leith and Dumbarton. The Union of 1603 led to the gradual pacification of the Border country and increased legitimate trade to England. The southern country had an inexhaustible need for meat, while the northern had an inexhaustible need for export earnings. The cattle trade was one of the driving forces leading to the Union of 1707, drawing the remoter parts of Scotland into the economic life of a united island. At the time of the Union, Scotland exported around 30,000 head of live cattle to England. In 1794, at the height of the boom caused by the Napoleonic Wars, it was estimated that three-quarters of the 100,000 cattle a year which passed through Smithfield were from north of the Border, though many were fattened on southern pastures. The war against France was won as much on Scotch beef as on the playing fields of Eton.

Cattle were cheaper to move by land than by sea because they did not have to carry their own food, and additionally

Bennachie Hill Fort

The hill fort on the Mither Tap overlooks the probable site of the Battle of Mons Graupius.
According to Tacitus the slopes were heavily forested then. The Caledonian army probably
descended from near the fort, to their nemesis below. (Walk 1, p22)

(IRM)

Roman Bath House, Bothwellhaugh

After the rigours of frontier patrols and route marches the Roman legionaries would have appreciated
the delights of the hot and cold baths at many of their permanent camps. The remains of this one
are found in Strathclyde Park and lie on the route of the Clyde Walkway (Walk 22, p126)

(IRM)

Glen Affric

The route through Glen Affric followed by St Duthac in the 11th century. Of course the road and the bridge were not there then, but Beinn Fhada (in the central background, with snow) was, and Duthac's route to Cada Duthac (Duthac's pass) and Loch Duich took the glen to the north (right) of the mountain. (Walk 4, p33)

(IRM)

Laggangairn Stones

On one of the several routes to Whithorn followed by pilgrim devotees of St Ninian. The stones, most of which have fallen, surround a mound, possibly a pre-Christian burial site. The remaining upright stones have been appropriated to Christian use, by the incision of the sign of the cross. (Walk 5, p42)

(IRM)

Carnmore

From Timothy Pont's drawings we know that he travelled past Carnmore, in a south-north direction from Poolewe to Dundonnell in the 1590s. This was a massive achievement, as James Hogg repeated the journey over 200 years later and stated that he could not have found his way without his local guide. (Walk 7, p53)

(IRM)

Culross Palace

John Taylor visited here on his great walk through Scotland in the early 1600s. It was the home of Sir George Bruce, much of whose fortune had come from coal mining in the area, including a mine under the Forth, reached by a mile long tunnel. You can follow Taylor's route over the Mounth (Walk 8, p53) but, alas, no longer his walk under the Forth.

(IRM)

Wade Bridge, Corrieyairack

A fine image of the bridge on the military road at the Laggan a' Bhainne, taken a century ago.
Fortunately it is still there, though the road itself is suffering from erosion and misuse. Built by the
Redcoats, the bridge was crossed by the Jacobite army on its way from Glenfinnan to Edinburgh.
(Walk 9, p63)
(AER/SMC)

Raiked Drove Road

The best remaining
raiked drove road, which,
unlike the military roads, is
not a scheduled ancient
monument, though it
certainly should be.
The braiding caused by
wandering cattle is
evident, and the finely
built drystane dykes are in
reasonable repair still.
Much work is needed to
restore and maintain this
unique relic of droving
days. (Walk 13, p84)
(IRM)

Corgarff Castle

The original fortified 16th century castle had the curtain wall added when it was garrisoned against the Jacobite threat. It remained occupied by troops after the '45 and until about 1830, troops mainly engaged in suppressing the illicit whisky trade, whose heartland was in the surrounding country of Upper Donside and Speyside. The castle contains an interesting display on the whisky trade. It lies near Walk 17, p104.

(IRM)

Hamish Dhu Macrae

The North East of Scotland was the centre of illicit distilling in its heyday, but the popular image of the trade is probably more represented by Hamish Dhu, the small scale operator hidden deep in the Highland hills, producing for a local market. This illustration dates from c.1905.

(AER/SMC)

Blackwater Graveyard

The resting place of the navvies who walked here, like Moleskin Joe from Greenock, to build the Blackwater Dam in the early 20th century, but who (unlike Joe) did not walk back out again when it was completed. It lies close to the site of their camp and rubbish tip. Another place that well merits protection by listing as an ancient Monument. (Walk 21, p125)

(IRM)

Summit Cairn, Firmounth Road

The reapers, shearers, drovers and whisky smugglers who used the Firmounth to cross from Deeside to the Mearns would have passed this cairn at the summit of the road. It commemorates the murder by a tinker of his wife at this spot. A local woman claimed to have given the couple milk before they ascended the pass. The tinker, who had previously denied ever being there, sealed his fate by responding, 'You old witch, it was only whey you gave.' (Walk 20, p115)

(IRM)

Central Station, Glasgow

Despite the efforts of time and developers, Central Station remains a Victorian industrial cathedral. Under its Umbrella (pictured) the Glasgow Gaels would shelter from the weather, and take strolls along Glasgow's streets. The Umbrella was so popular that it was denounced in sermons as attracting people away from church on Sundays. (Walk 23, p137)

(IRM)

Aberdeen Hunger Marchers

The Aberdeen contingent heading along Union Street, still with its trams and cassies (cobbles), on their 500 mile walk to London, the longest of any contingent in the marches of the 1930s. Headed by their pipers (pictured) the Aberdeen contingent had the place of honour at the head, as the march entered the capital.

(Source Unknown)

Gypsy Palace, Kirk Yetholm

The palace was the residence of the Gypsy Kings and Queens in the 19th century, but was built at a time when the gypsy lifestyle was already in decline, and they were slowly being integrated into mainstream living. By the 1880s the Palace was a tourist attraction. It stands on Muggers Row, the street where the gypsies had their residences for centuries, and from which they fled to England in times of trouble. (Walk 25, p153) they provided their own transport – firstly to the lowland trysts at Crieff, Falkirk or Dumfries, where they were sold, and secondly southwards to the fattening fields and final market. To the trysts they came on the drove roads from the western and central Highlands, as well as from Galloway and Ireland, and from the lowlands of the North East. To call these routes 'roads' is possibly misleading. Certainly drove roads would have followed existing tracks through glens and over passes, but cattle cannot be driven in a line like ponies, and they wandered, partly to graze. This led to the widening and 'braiding' of drove roads, which can be seen clearly on the Monega Pass amongst the present-day droves of skiers at the Cairnwell, as well as on the ancient cattle route south of Peebles in the Borders. The passage of the cattle would undoubtedly have worsened these tracks, as anyone who has walked a hill path used by cattle, especially after wet weather, can testify.

There is a myth that the cattle disliked the new military and later parliamentary roads, as they hurt their feet. But in actual fact cattle were generally shod for the drove, shoes made in Crossgates being especially favoured, and before the introduction of tarmacadam, road surfaces were not appreciably harder on feet than many a rough hill pass such as the Lairig an Laoigh in the Cairngorms. Where the beasts were driven away from the constructed roads, it was usually as much an attempt to avoid paying tolls or to ensure supplies of grazing as anything to do with protecting the feet of the beasts. Telford's new parliamentary road through Glen Moriston, for example, was regularly used by the drovers, as it saved them a full day's journey on the old route.

Since bridges were associated with tolls, and because cattle tend to panic on a bridge, herds were more often than not swum across water. Sometimes this was unavoidable, as at Kylerhea between Skye and the mainland. There, a noose was put round each cow's jaw, and tied to the tail of the cow in front; in strings of six or eight they were swum across. Drovers, skilled at such passages, would thus find avoiding a toll bridge on a river easy work. (As well as avoiding tolls as far as possible, drovers kept clear of bandit country – until well into the 18th century the areas around Barrisdale in Knoydart and Lochaber were especially dangerous.)

A day's journey was from 10 to 12 miles. Cattle needed to graze and to drink en route to avoid losing condition, and the drovers had to stop at places (called 'stances') where they were assured of water and grazing for their beasts at night. There is a wonderful green sward at the head of Glen Tanar which was a drovers' stance, and 10 miles or so south in Glen Esk lies another. The dung deposited by the animals increased soil fertility and was one of the reasons why, initially, there was little opposition to the right of passage of the drovers and their beasts. In the lowlands and Southern Uplands it was different. Drove roads (called 'raiks') were constructed with dykes to keep the beasts off cropland. For the cattle it was a long journey to their deaths; depending on where they originated, the journey to the fattening and killing fields could take, at 10 miles a day, from upwards of one month to almost two. For the drovers the journey took longer, as they had to return.

Some of the entrepreneurial drovers rode to market with their beasts. Cameron of Corriechoillie, dubbed the 'King of the Drovers', certainly rode to the Falkirk trysts he attended. Like the others who were mounted, he would probably have gone ahead to arrange the night's food and grazing. However, Cameron's men would have walked the whole way from the

Western Highlands, or from North East Scotland, to the cattle fairs at Crieff. (After 1750, the fairs were usually held at Falkirk, which was more convenient for the southern middlemen.) The drovers were generally driving the beasts of others (landlords and middlemen), but some would drive a beast or two of their own, or be hired to take a neighbour's animal (individual beasts were often sold to pay a tenant's rent). And the droves were huge, like later Wild West round-ups. Droves over a mile long could be seen in the Drumochter Pass, and herds of more than 1,000 cattle were collected at Dalwhinnie.

The trysts must have been colourful and noisy affairs. Imagine thousands of beasts bellowing and bleating, collies barking, and shouts in Gaelic, Scots and English from the hundreds of people camped around in primitive tents, cooking their food and engaging in conviviality. At these trysts not only beasts were traded; men were hired to take them south to England. Many would therefore be away from their homes from May until October, often seeking harvest work in the south before returning. A drove was as long as a piece of string – for some it was of a few weeks' duration; for others it lasted several months. (Scott's wonderful tale 'The Two Drovers', although fiction, gives a realistic account of droving life.)

The drovers led eventful lives and were colourful characters. Macky, an observer at the Crieff Tryst in 1723, where 30,000 cattle were sold for as many guineas, gave a detailed description of the drovers. Noting that they were 'mighty civil', he said that they wore a belted plaid down to the knee, and a bonnet and stockings 'of striped stuff' – probably tartan. They carried arms, usually a broadsword with a knife and pistol, and were exempt from the Disarming Acts which followed the Rebellions of 1715 and '45. Illustrations of the drovers universally show them wearing shoes and stockings, so bare-kneed they might have been, but not bare-footed. They travelled light and, aside from their clothes and arms, carried meagre rations. The staple of their diet was oatmeal, mixed with water and cooked if possible, eaten cold if not. Additionally a supply of onions appears to have varied the diet, and whisky seems to have been their favoured drink. Observers also comment, sometimes in a horrified manner, on the habit some drovers had of bleeding their cattle and mixing the blood with oatmeal to make a primitive, and doubtless nourishing, pudding.

It was reported of the drovers that though they might stop at stances where there were inns, they seldom spent the night inside. This might partly have been to save money, but mainly it was done to watch over the cattle and prevent them from straying. Drovers were observed, after spending a night in the open under their plaids, to rise and brush the hoar frost off their clothes and exposed body parts, without apparently feeling any ill-effects. For this epic of endurance they were hired at one shilling a day in the early 18th century, which rose to three or four shillings in the war boom of the 1790s. But the drover had to find his way home at his own expense.

It is often assumed that the first Highlander any Englishman saw was in the 1745 Rebellion, but droving shows this not to be the case. On both the east coast, and the west coast routes followed by the Jacobites in 1745, the sight of large numbers of men in Highland dress and speaking Gaelic must have been a common sight in many parts of rural England. At one drover to 50 animals, it took many men to bring the cattle to market. Despite its reiving origins, droving gained a reputation for honesty, and in Skye drovers' bills circulated as currency. Not all drovers were Highlanders, and many came from lowland Aberdeenshire for the long trek south. The canny men of the North East did not disdain manual labour, as did the Celt, and they knitted stockings and gloves as they walked, selling these fashionable products of the Aberdeenshire woollen industry on their way south. But the strangest sight associated with droving must have been that of the collie dogs going home.

Dogs are the unsung heroes of droving, and the drover always saw to his dog before attending to his own needs at a stop. They herded the cattle in the way they later, much more famously, herded the sheep. Once the drove was over the drover might take seasonal work, and he sent the collie home. Finding its way by smell and knowledge, the dog would arrive back long before its master. On the way north, the intelligent animal would stop and be fed at inns passed on the way south. Next year the drover would pay the reckoning with the landlord. How the dogs must have loved the trip!

Gradually the life of a drover became less dangerous as bandit depredations upon the stock declined to a marginal element. However, other problems soon arose. Rights of grazing on common land dated from the Middle Ages, but with the enclosure movement there was less land available. Additionally, land which had been marginal, and benefited from the dung of passing cattle, became valuable for grazing sheep or, more importantly, deer. Landlords often attempted to dispute the right of passage through the glens to cattle, and though they invariably lost these claims, the House of Lords in 1848 ruled that free grazing violated the laws of property. Increasingly, charges were imposed upon beasts at stances which were formerly free, and these had to be paid out of the drovers' winnings.

Further factors led to the decline of droving. The

improvement of stock, such as the development of the Aberdeen Angus strain, favoured the rearers of the eastern lowlands, whose cattle became more in demand than the rugged, but leaner, Highland beast. In the 1840s cattle began to be shipped by steamer from Aberdeen at £1 a head, a much cheaper business than droving. The railway network dealt a death blow to the droving trade, and from Aberdeen in 1888 and 1889, 1,000 cattle a month headed south by train to London. In the middle of the century over 100,000 cattle a year were assembled at the three Falkirk Trysts, but by 1880 this had declined to 15,000 and droving had become a folk-loric relic. Eyewitnesses from the late 19th century describe the last drovers as 'shaggy and uncultured' and 'dressed in homespun so thick they looked like bears', many appearing to have been 'old men' – descriptions in marked contrast to those of earlier quoted observers. Droving continued on a tiny scale; Seton Gordon recalls meeting some Knoydart men passing into Glen Dessary with a herd of cattle in the 1930s. The cattle have largely gone, and the bracken has spread on former grazings; and the poor collies now have nothing to herd but silly, bleating sheep.

Suggested Walks

WALK 13

Peebles to St Mary's Loch (OS 73)

Probably the best surviving example of a raik or walled in drovers' road, which prevented the cattle straying onto cultivated farmland. At Peebles the drovers were liable to pay customs duty as they passed south, and in return had grazing rights at Kingsmuir in the town.

South of Peebles the Gypsy Glen leads to the easily followed route, which ascends (enclosed by drystane dykes) over Kailzie Hill, Kirkhope Law and Birkskairn Hill, with the higher Dun Rig looming to the west. From the watershed the route descends towards the Yarrow past Blackhouse where James Hogg was once a shepherd. From thence a farm road leads down to the A703. The Gordon Arms, with its Hogg and Walter Scott associations, is about a mile east of here and should not be missed.

Peebles to the Gordon Arms Hotel: 14 miles, 7 hours.

WALK 14

Loch Arkaig to Glengarry by Fedden (OS 34)

Drovers took this route from Skye to Fort William, as it saved a day on the route via Invergarry. At Tomdoun, where there was a drovers' inn and there still is a hotel, was formerly a stance where the cattle trails from Knoydart and Skye merged. The cattle then swam the narrows at Garrygulach, but the pedestrian is advised to cross by the bridge down-stream from the hotel at Torr-na Carraidh, before proceeding to Greenfield. Carry on east to the Allt Ladiadh, which is crossed by another bridge, before the route turns south, and then heads through the woods till the watershed at the ruin of Fedden is reached. Here the cattle and drovers overnighted. Fedden is a corruption of *fheadain*, meaning in Gaelic 'a chanter', and is so called from the way the wind howls through the pass here. The notorious outlaw Ewan Macphee found refuge here for a while in the early 19th century, and on the slopes of the neighbouring Meall an Tagraidh another fugitive, Bonnie Prince Charlie, also hid out on his own earlier wanderings. From Fedden a good path goes down Gleann Cia-aig to the splendid waterfalls, where it meets the B8006 at the Dark Mile.

Tomdoun to the Dark Mile: 15 miles, 8 hours.

CHAPTER 8

The Pedestrian Pursuit
of Knowledge

BEFORE 1750 FEW LOWLAND Scots or English ventured into the Highlands unless on a military expedition. By 1800 tourists were arriving in numbers, but so also men engaged on work of a scientific nature. Amongst these were several walkers of note, who wore out hides of leather in pursuit of their intellectual passions.

The pacification of the Highlands was followed by cartographic surveys. The maps of Major General William Roy, completed 1747–52 for the Ordnance Office, gave a sketch of the lie of the Scottish mainland in case of any future rebellions. Later the Ordnance Survey undertook the mapping of the whole of the British Isles on a six inch scale. The extension of the work in Scotland was the initiative of Colonel, later Major General, Thomas Colby, Director General of the OS from 1820 to '46. There can be little doubt that Colby is the most prodigious pedestrian ever to have trodden Scottish soil. He was a man of incredible stamina and fanatical addiction to his work. His field journals were lost when the Luftwaffe bombed the OS in World War II. However, a unique account of Colby at work survives in the form of a letter by OS Major Dawson, one of Colby's subordinates, from the year 1819. That year was one of walking wonders; a pedestrian *annus mirabilis*.

Colby's toughness awed Dawson, who describes how

Colby had arrived at 'Huntley' after having travelled from London by mail coach in the driver's box, since 'neither rain nor snow, nor any degree of severity in the weather' would have made Colby sit inside the coach or even use a scarf. Colby was able to travel for days and nights without stopping and 'with but little refreshment, and that of the plainest kind'. On the top of Corriehabbie Hill south west of Huntly, the OS party built a village of turf and stone hovels with tarpaulin roofs, for living and sleeping in while they worked. Much of the materials had to be carried on the men's backs when the horses found the ground too difficult. However, those at base camp were in luxury when compared to the men engaged in field surveys.

The journeys of Colby and his men are impressive enough, but we should remember that they were also surveying as they walked, carrying heavy measuring equipment and engaging in note-taking and sketching. Some nights they stayed in hotels of a sort (at 'a miserable mud hovel' in Cluanie they slept on chairs and had stale salmon for sustenance). Other nights they camped under canvas. Once, near Dingwall, they were 'glad to eat a mess of oatmeal, mixed with cold water, and sleep in a blanket upon the baggage'. Colby had developed a method of movement akin to that later used in commando training:

> Captain Colby having ascertained the general direction by means of a pocket compass and map, the whole party set off as on a steeplechase, running down the mountain at full speed... crossing glens, wading streams and regardless of all difficulties that were not actually insurmountable on foot.

Colby and his subordinates made two epic journeys on foot

in the summer of 1819. The first was through eastern Invernesshire, Rosshire, Caithness and Orkney, and occupied 22 days of walking totalling 513 miles – and they were measuring, so the distances are not open to question. Back at Corriehabbie, Colby allowed his men one day of rest and they set off again. In a further 22 days they walked westwards to Kintail and Skye, crossing back to Wester Ross and returning to base camp. This time the mileage was 586. On these 44 days they were engaged in the arduous work of cartography as well as undertaking their daily walking stint. Furthermore, they were climbing mountains in order to ascertain their heights trigonometrically. Slioch in Wester Ross and one of the Five Sisters in Kintail were among those ascended by them; the surveyors climbed a mountain every third or fourth day. There were some weather-enforced rest days that chaffed Colby's patience, but for which his men were grateful. Over their two trips, the OS men on hill and glen averaged 25 miles a day; take out the bad weather days and we are nearer an average of 30 miles. In my opinion no modern walker could rival this month and a half of continuous exertion of more than 1,100 miles, with the ascent of over a dozen peaks thrown in.

Dawson remarks that Colby was able to bear the labours of his surveying easily, but some of his men found it harder. On the first day from Corriehabbie, the party walked (or rather jogged) 39 miles to arrive at Aviemore. The next day, Dawson was 'dreadfully stiff', and after 13 miles begged Colby to allow him to proceed to that night's destination by road, rather than following his leader over the Monadhliath mountains. 'I petitioned strongly to be excused from accompanying him, but he would not excuse me... judging... from accurate observation and long experience, and he was right.' Dawson crossed the mountains, arriving at Garviemore near midnight after travelling 40 miles that day, and feeling fresher than when he had started out. Colby must have had a heart after all, for next day the trigonometers took it easy, and they only walked a further 24 miles – although they did climb a mountain of over 3,500 feet en route. Of all the hardships they faced, the cartographers found the midges most difficult to bear, commenting that, 'We had frequently to make smoke in our bedrooms, and over our meals, to drive these insects away.'

Dawson says the men wore coats, waistcoats and shirts for their work; nothing out of the civilian ordinary – in 1819 Macintosh's waterproof garments were still five years away. Some of the time the men travelled by good roads. They crossed the old Wade road over the Corrieyairack Pass, which was in regular use for carriages at this time, and Dawson also mentions moving up the Great Glen by 'the line of one of the old military roads of General Roy' (meaning, presumably, a road marked on Roy's map, for it was a Wade road). Interestingly, they then took 'the parliamentary road, made by the late Mr Telford' towards Cluanie through Glen Moriston. Between 1804 and 1824, Telford built over 900 miles of roads in the Highlands. Much of the time, however, the OS men would have been on rough drove roads or coffin tracks, like the Coulin Pass they crossed to Torridon.

Colby was a hard taskmaster, but he fed his men well – victuals are mentioned frequently in Dawson's account of the 1819 journeys. It was a heavy diet of protein and carbohydrates: broth, meat, bread, oatmeal porridge, salmon and game were common constituents. The final celebration back at Corriehabbie in September, on completion of the summer's work, indicates the kind of nutrients they normally consumed (though in smaller portions). 'Success to the Trig' was toasted, and a plum pudding ('ordinary hill fare,' as Dawson describes it) of 100 pounds in weight was made, which took 20 hours to cook. 'The approved proportions of the ingredients being – a pound of raisins, a pound of currants, a pound of suet etc to each pound of flour; these quantities were all multiplied by the amount of mouths in the camp...'

There exists but one man to my knowledge who might have been able to equal Colby's feats of prodigious pedestrianism. William MacGillivray was born in Aberdeen in 1796, the illegitimate son of a local woman and a Highland soldiering father who disappeared. He was brought up by an uncle in Harris, but came back to study at Aberdeen University. He became Professor of Natural History in Aberdeen from 1841 until his death in 1852. As a naturalist, MacGillivray was one of the leading men of his generation. Darwin admired 'the accurate MacGillivray', and the latter collaborated with the great American naturalist John James Audubon in the *History of British Birds* of 1837, where birds are, for the first time, classified according to anatomical structure. MacGillivray was an outstanding example of the humble 'lad o' pairts' who helped contribute much to the scientific reputation of Scotland.

MacGillivray became a strong walker early in life, born of necessity given his poverty. At the age of 11 he took the boat from Harris to the mainland and then walked to Aberdeen to begin his studies – almost 200 miles. While a student at Aberdeen, he would walk home to spend the summers on the island. The direct route from Aberdeen to the Western Isles goes via Elgin to Inverness, but in 1817 MacGillivray took a longer and more arduous route, walking to Braemar and crossing the Cairngorms by the Lairig Ghru before reaching the Highland capital. Thereafter he tramped to Achnasheen, before passing alongside Loch Maree to Gairloch and the boat. It rained incessantly, and on one occasion MacGillivray passed the night in a damp cave by Loch Maree.

The motivation for MacGillivray's trips home was to live cheaply during the summertime. The reason for his epic trip to London in 1819 was the pursuit of scientific knowledge. As a student at Aberdeen, he desired to study the natural history collections in the British Museum:

> In London city there is, I am told a great collection... of all the creatures which have been found upon the face of the earth. Thither, therefore, I shall direct my steps...

Lacking the wherewithal for a return ticket by sea, he walked south in the same year as Colby walked north and west. However, MacGillivray virtually doubled the distance to London to over 800 miles by crossing the Cairngorms to Ben Nevis, and then walking south through the Lake District to London, annotating, classifying, observing as he went – and writing a journal of his trip. He was a firm believer in the naturalist getting his boots dubby, and commented that, 'The naturalist must not shut himself up in his study while the wintry winds blow over the blasted heath,' denouncing 'cabinet naturalists' and making himself more enemies.

With him on this trip MacGillivray carried 10 pounds in cash and a knapsack (measuring 18 inches by 14) made of oiled cloth, which cost him two shillings and sixpence and contained his paper, maps, books, ink, paints and toiletries. Clothing consisted of a coat, trousers, vest, shirt, hat and gloves, two pairs of socks and a pair of stout shoes. At first he walked 30 miles each day, but he did not maintain this pace. His route took him to Fort William and then south to Glasgow, where he visited the Botanic Gardens. Further walking took him to Ayr, Stranraer and Dumfries, before he crossed into England. He approached London with relief, carrying out two stretches of 51 and 58 miles with nothing but bread and an apple: 'My shoes and stockings were in tatters so the gravel was getting in and tormenting me.' To make matters worse, for the last 12 hours it poured with rain. He had walked 837 miles in about 50 days by the time he arrived in London. He spent seven days in the city, sightseeing and studying, and then sailed home to Aberdeen, a wretched 10 days' journey of seasickness which left him physically and mentally exhausted. But he had made up his mind as to a career, commenting that 'it will go hard with me if I do not one day merit the name of ornithologist.'

MacGillivray carried out many other long walks in his scientific investigations, which focused on the Cairngorm area. The results were embodied in his masterpiece *The Natural History of Deeside*, which was published after his death in 1856 with funds provided by Queen Victoria. He crossed to Speyside from Deeside several times, including a traverse by the plateau of Braeriach, and he went over to the Linn o' Dee in 1816 'across the mountains from Blair in Athol', most probably via Glen Tilt. Though he was a very strong walker, MacGillivray was in no hurry, stopping to sketch or shoot specimens, or to make notes or observe the fauna. Thus, though he travelled huge distances, he never rivalled the pace set by Colby. On his journeys MacGillivray was ill-equipped – very often he had no map, no compass, nor even a watch. It is clear that frequently he did not know where he was, and very often the names of mountains he climbed were not known to him. He ascended Beinn a'

Bhuird in 1819, and only discovered the name of the hill when a local informed him the following day.

His main interest was scientific, and although MacGillivray loved mountain scenery he was not prepared for the rigours of the hill. He was naturally strong, but a life of sleeping rough on the heather, frequently wet, and living on a pock of oatmeal with only water to drink, undermined his system. A typical comment in one of his journals records: 'Came to Dubrach tenanted by MacHardy, who, expressing his concern at my having been out all night, treated me to a glass of whisky and some bread and milk.' Such parsimony affected his performance on the hills. In 1819 he slept out in the Garbh Choire of Braeriach, making a bed from heather and grass, putting on his gloves, sipping some water and nibbling a little cheese before trying to sleep. On proceeding the next day, he confesses, 'Before I got to the base of the rocks I felt very weak and was obliged to stop every now and then.' We can excuse a naturalist writing almost 200 years ago for being ignorant of the essential connection between nutrition and bodily strength. On Lochnagar in 1850, he contracted what we would now call hypothermia and died two years later.

As a Highlander, MacGillivray hated the Clearances and the resulting sheep economy, and the extermination of 'vermin' to protect blood sports, noting, 'The same inconsiderable selfishness which has cleared Van Diemen's land of its original population had destroyed our magnificent Eagles and sagacious Ravens.' He also regretted the transport revolution – the steamers and trains which, by his death, had popularised the glens and made the walking that he had undertaken in the course of his work no longer a necessity.

Suggested Walks

WALK 15

The Lairig Ghru (os 36 and 43)

MacGillivray was only one of many who crossed this pass. It is a long and hard route, one of the hardest in this book, and not everyone who tried has made it. Clach nan Taillear commemorates the spot where a group of tailors crossing the pass for a bet met their deaths, and they have not been the only ones to suffer this fate in the Lairig. The path goes very high, to about 2,700 ft, and requires settled weather. Though it was a drove road, the drovers didn't take their calves over here, instead using the lower Lairig an Laoigh (Calves Pass) further east.

Start at Braemar, or if transport can be arranged, at the Linn o' Dee. Take the path to the White Brig and the Chest o' Dee and then follow the path on the east side of the river Dee, not the unsightly Land Rover track on the west. The NTS, which now owns Mar Estate, is committed to removing this scar. As you head north towards the pass the scenery becomes magnificent, with the Devil's Point visible. Across the river lies Corrour Bothy, useable for an overnight or emergency shelter. It was originally a deer watcher's bothy, built in 1875. Just north of here is the Clach na Taillear, and the track rises steeply thence towards the Pools of Dee and the stony summit of the pass. The descent to Rothiemurchus and its delightful pine woods is straightforward, and the public road starts at Coylumbridge, with a further couple of miles to Aviemore, and bus and train links north and south.

Linn o' Dee to Coylumbridge: 22 miles, 12 hours.
Braemar to Aviemore: 30 miles, 15 hours.

WALK 16

The ascent of Mam Sodhail to the OS station (OS 25)

Colby and his men climbed Slioch – amongst other mountains – but the ascent of Mam Sodhail in Glen Affric allows you to see the best extant remains of an OS mountain station. The men of the OS occupied the summit from 29 July to 31 August 1848, and there are extensive signs of their stay. Under Colonel Winzer their efforts estimated the mountain's height at 3,862 ft. He commented in the Account of the Principal Triangulation that, 'the station is on the highest point of the mountain, and is marked by a stone pile 23 feet high and 60 feet in circumference.' This huge cairn is still there and a little below it is the remains of their bothy, which was built with a door and windows – and a fireplace. When I slept in the ruin, it contained a broken skillet, as well as an old leather sole with nail holes. Just below the ruin is the clear outline of the latrine which the men dug for their stay.

Their ascent would have gone by the present Affric Lodge (not built in 1848), and along Loch Affric to, probably, the col south of Mam Sodhail by Coire Leachavie and the Allt Corie Leachavie.

Affric Lodge to the OS station: 6 miles (7 from the Glen Affric road end), 4 hours.

CHAPTER 9

Distillers and Gaugers

IF THE CATTLE TRADE was one of the major forces behind the Union of 1707, the whisky trade almost led to the Union's dissolution in 1713. From 1760–1830, drovers and distillers often used the same glens and presented varied images of picturesque convoys to an observer; however, while the drover was on legitimate business, the distiller was engaged in a desperate struggle with the law.

Whisky has been distilled in Scotland from about the 15th century, but by the 18th century it had become the national drink. The private distilling and consumption of whisky was legal in Scotland, but its sale was not. Distilleries were licensed and some were large-scale. The problem was that after the Union, as a price for access to English colonial markets, Scots had to accept a share of England's tax burden – a bargain which the Scots found, according to the impeccable national illogic, unreasonable.

In 1713 the malt tax was extended into Scotland – which led to such outrage that a measure for the repeal of the Treaty of Union was defeated by only four votes in the House of Lords. The implementation of the tax in 1725 caused riots in Glasgow, with several deaths. The tax, along with the tax on the spirit itself, meant that large distilleries that were open to excise inspection were at a disadvantage, compared with small law-breaking distillers in remote areas. John Stein, a lowland distiller, stated in 1797 that 'owing to the interference of Highland spirits, we have been unable to find sales'. The only legitimate distiller able to compete was Duncan Forbes of Culloden, who had prevented many from joining the Jacobites in 1745–6, and had had his distillery at Ferintosh burnt by the rebels. As reward from a grateful government, he was exempt from the duty on spirits. When in 1784 this concession was revoked, Burns spoke for the nation:

Thee, Ferintosh, O sadly lost
Scotland lament frae coast tae coast
Now colic grips and barkin hoast
may kill us a'

For Burns and for many Scots, whisky went not only with freedom, but with good health. One exciseman agreed with Burns, noting in 1736 that 'the ruddy complexion and strength of these people is not owing to water-drinking, but to the *aqua vitae*.'

The whisky trade spread like wildfire, especially in the north eastern upland plateau between the Highlands and the available markets in the lowlands. Figures prove the point: in 1822 there were almost 10,000 people prosecuted for breaking the excise laws in Aberdeen and Elgin courts alone, amounting to over two thirds of total Scottish prosecutions. There were over 200 active stills in Glenlivet in about 1800, and Tomintoul was described 15 years later as 'a wild mountain village, where drinking, dancing and swearing went on all the time'. The Cabrach was another lawless area, with 200 active stills. By the 1760s it was estimated that 90 per cent of all Scottish whisky sales were illicit, and an observer commented that the trade had 'spread over the whole face of the country, where the face of an Exciseman is never seen'. Controlling the trade was also difficult because many landlords connived at it, since the money it brought in ensured that their tenants could pay their rents. After the '45, soldiers were stationed at places like Braemar and Corgarff castles, and once the residual Jacobites were hunted down the soldiery became primarily involved in excise duties, aiding the gaugers in their thankless struggles.

During the period when the distillers were winning their war with the gaugers, the smuggling trade was highly organised, and ingenious methods were used. Women walking with their wares to market in neighbouring towns would acquire miraculous pregnancies; inflated bladders full of the whisky which they would deliver or sell to customers. Innocent-looking parties on coffin tracks, walking to the cemetery and resting awhile from the labour of carrying their burden, might well be over-refreshed – not from drowning their sorrows at the loss of the supposed deceased, but because the coffin held supplies of whisky for delivery to consumers. In some kirks a portion of the gallery was known as the 'smugglers' loft', where they would sit holding their heads high because they could easily pay their pew-rent. The local lairds' connivance at smuggling was shown by the low penalties imposed in areas where illicit distilling was endemic: while the fine in Fife or Ayr was the statutory £20, at Aberdeen capture and conviction would cost you on average 11s and 3d. One JP in a North East court was embarrassed when the accused said to him, 'I havnae made a drap since yon wee keg I sent tae yersel.' Fines were often paid by the smuggling community from a levy.

The main method of delivery of illicit whisky was a well-organised armed convoy. Once the amber dew had been distilled, it was poured into barrels (called 'akers') and these were set on panniers over a pony. A long string of ponies was tied together by their tails and noses, and they proceeded to walk, accompanied by 20 or 30 men, on the outward journey to their destination – then the men would ride back home on the empty animals. Accounts speak of how heavily armed the smugglers were, carrying cudgels, swords and pistols. The whisky convoy was accompanied by dogs, which would have been excellent lookouts, picking up the sound and scent of any unwelcome persons along the way. The convoy would have maintained a faster pace than the drovers, with ponies able to cover greater distances in a day's walk than cattle, and not having to graze on the way. Nevertheless, the journey from the Cabrach or Glenlivet to the Mearns, Strathmore or the Laigh o' Moray, was one that occupied two or three days' or (as often as not) nights' walking for the smugglers. Stealth was at least as important for the smugglers as speed, and they utilised the less-frequented whisky roads through and over the mountains.

The military road from Tomintoul goes by the Lecht to Corgarff, and the main drove road south from Tomintoul and Glenlivet goes by Inchrory to Deeside and then southwards. But the main route used by smugglers started in the Braes o' Glenlivet and went over the Ladder Hills by Ladderfoot, thence descending to Bellabeg on Donside. Following the route today, you pass the ruin of 'Duffdefiance', where a man evicted from Glenlivet for illicit distilling in the early 19th century walked over the hills, built a house, and had the lum reekin' – thus claiming squatter's rights – before Duff (the laird defied) could evict him.

From Bellabeg the convoy would have moved, probably by night, through the populated district of Cromar, before arriving at Aboyne and starting the next stage of their journey over the Fungle Road the following day. Formerly the Cattrin Road, named from its reiver days, this was an established drove road which the smugglers followed over the hill to Tarfside in Glenesk. Thereafter, the law-abiding drovers followed the North Esk to Fettercairn and then to market. But the smugglers walked their ponies another route south, through the less frequented Clash of Wirren to Glen Lethnot, and then south by Brigend to the track between the Brown and White Caterthuns (Iron Age hill forts), from which vantage point (and splendid camp) they waited for night to fall, to descend upon Brechin. This was the route known as the 'Whisky Road'.

Smugglers and drovers also took different routes elsewhere. While they may have crossed the Cairn o' Mount together from Deeside, at the Clatterin Brig they thereafter parted ways, the distillers taking a back route behind Fasque to avoid the gaugers. A place thereabouts is called 'Donald's Bed', where a murdered exciseman lay for 20 years before discovery – showing that at least one of their number had been, unhappily, wise to the smugglers' trick.

Whatever problems they encountered on the whisky roads, the smugglers knew none that compared with the terrors experienced by the exciseman. His was an unpopular and dangerous job, and it is not surprising that many took the easy option and turned a blind eye to smuggling. However, professional pride and the bounties attendant upon seizure of contraband provoked many into actions of incredible heroism. The 'King of the Gaugers' must have been Malcolm Gillespie, who for 28 years harassed the smugglers of Aberdeenshire. In that time he impounded 6,535 gallons of whisky, 407 stills, 165 horses, 85 carts and 62,400 gallons of barley wash. Gillespie trained dogs to tumble horses, and his men were armed with swords and pistols, which they unfailingly used. He himself sustained 42 wounds in his career and was battered near to death on frequent occasions. His reward from the state he served was to be hanged for circulating forged bills in 1827.

Some of Gillespie's exploits are the stuff of legend. A party of smugglers set out from Upper Deeside on one occasion, with ten cartloads of whisky and a numerous armed guard. It was night, and a fearful one, so the smugglers expected no exciseman to be abroad. They reached Culter without opposition, where the gaugers lay in ambush, and a battle ensued between the two sides. In the end the smugglers fled, leaving several wounded and one of their men dead, and the whisky fell into Gillespie's hands.

But the battles were not always won by the gaugers, as is recorded in the ballad 'The Battle of Corrymuckloch', which describes an encounter that took place around 1820 between some smugglers and excisemen supported by soldiers of the Royal Scots Greys. The contraband had come to Glen Quoich in Perthshire when the smugglers were accosted by the armed soldiery. Using sticks – and a dyke for missiles – they put the soldiers ('the beardies') to flight and captured the exciseman:

But Donald and his men stuck fast
An garr'd the beardies quit the field
The gauger he was thumped weel
Afore his pride would lat him yield

And sometimes the gaugers simply, and wisely, declined combat. The Rev Thomas Guthrie wrote that as a boy in Brechin in the early years of the 19th century, the sight of men 'come down from the wilds of Aberdeenshire or the glens of the Grampians' carrying their whisky on 'small, shaggy but brave and hardy steeds' was common. He confirms that they watched 'on some commanding eminence' (probably one of the Caterthuns) during the day, and only moved onto the plains at night, distributing their whisky 'to agents they had everywhere'. And for the smugglers, there was nothing like rubbing the outnumbered and defeated enemy's nose in the dirt, as Guthrie noted:

> I have seen a troop of thirty of them riding in Indian file, and in broad day, though the streets of Brechin, after they had succeeded in disposing of their whisky, and they rode leisurely along, beating time with their formidable cudgels on the empty barrels to the great amusement of the public and the mortification of the excisemen, who had nothing for it but to bite their nails and stand, as best they could, the raillery of the smugglers and the laughter of the people.

Eventually the government was compelled to deal rigorously with a trade which resulted in so much lost revenue. By 1822 agents for the excise were assisting at trials, imposing the minimum penalty of a £20 fine or six months in prison, with transportation for those who violently resisted arrest. The increased success of military-backed seizures is testified to by the 6,000 cases tried in that year. In 1823 the duty on whisky was reduced to 2s 3d per gallon, giving the advantage back to licensed distillers with their economies of scale. In addition, tenants found guilty of illicit distilling were evicted. By 1832 less than 200 cases concerning illicit distilling were heard in Scottish courts. 'Poachers', like John Begg on Deeside and George Smith in Glenlivet, turned 'gamekeepers' and set up commercial production. The new status of whisky was demonstrated by the presentation of a bottle by Sir Walter Scott to King George IV on his visit to Edinburgh in 1822. The ending of the illicit industry led to massive depopulation on upper Donside, the Cabrach and Glenlivet. The trade survived only in really remote Highland locations.

James Mitchell records that as he was taking a drive up

Glen Moriston sometime before 1825, 'I saw before me at some little distance about twenty five Highland horses tied to each other, and carrying two kegs of whisky each.' The men walking with the ponies were in bonnets and plaids, carrying bludgeons. They recognised Mitchell and, instead of beating him, offered him a dram.

In the 1840s, driven by hunger, a Kintail Macrae walked 20 miles to Loch Monar and built a house on an island. There he and his son Hamish made illicit whisky on a scale large enough to live off. They walked to fairs in Beauly and Dingwall to sell the product, and when the elder Macrae died he was carried in his coffin back to Kintail by bearers on foot. In the early years of the 20th century, now an old man with the gaugers closing in, Hamish walked out of the glen to end his days in an old folk's home. But not before he carried out his last trick, the old illicit distiller's one of turning in his ancient equipment to the gauger for the reward.

Suggested Walks

WALK 17

Glenlivet to Donside, by the Ladder Road (os 36 and 37)

The Braes o' Glenlivet are reached by a side road off the B9008 north of Tomintoul. If time permits, a trip to Scalan, where there was a secret Catholic seminary in bygone days, is worthwhile.

From Chapeltown the route goes by Corry and then steeply up the Ladder Burn to the summit below Dun Muir. It then descends through boggy ground to one of the far too many bulldozed tracks in this area, which in turn drops down to Duffdefiance. Here Lucky Thain is reputed to have lived, though to me this ruin looks like a sheep farm from a later date and the ruin visible nearer the Nochty Water is a more likely location for the illicit still. A song, 'The Battle of Glen Nochty', commemorates a shoot out between gaugers and distillers here. The route now enters the woods and attains Aldachuie, where the famous Lost Gallery (refreshments) is situated. The track then continues down Glen Nochty to the minor road which in turn takes you to Bellabeg. Time and transport permitting, it is worth visiting Corgarff Castle west of Bellabeg, where there is much information on the days of illicit distilling on Donside.

From Chapeltown to Aldachuie: 9 miles, 5 hours.

To Bellabeg: 13 miles, 7 hours.

WALK 18

Tarfside to the Caterthuns (OS 44)

With an overnight stay at Tarfside, this walk could be combined with No. 8, or No. 20, in either direction. Drovers who reached Tarfside in Glen Esk by the various routes from Deeside moved down the easy terrain of the River Tarf to their destinations. The distillers took this back road for concealment, and it was known locally as the Whisky Road.

From Tarfside the route ascended Cowie Hill and then skirted East Knock to the Clash of Wirren (*clais fuaran* means 'hollow of the springs' in Gaelic), and then down to the Westwater and Stoneyford. Do not cross here, but remain on the north, then east side of the West Water. From Stoneyford, the next couple of miles is rough and not easy to follow, but at Craig of Finnoch you come to the remains of what was to have been an engineered road over the Mounth over 200 years ago, and the going is good till Drumcairn. From Bridgend to the Caterthuns is on a public road, though a quiet one.

Tarfside to Bridgend: 11 miles, 5 hours; to the Caterthuns: 13 miles, 6 hours.

CHAPTER 10

Women Walking, Mostly

THE WALKING TALES of war, scientific exploration and commerce outlined thus far have involved men. That women were capable of pedestrian achievements is suggested by the fictional account given in Scott's *Heart of Midlothian* of Jeanie Deans' barefoot walk from Edinburgh to London in the early 18th century, seeking a pardon for her sister. There are many examples from real life to show that Jeanie's feat on foot was not beyond her sisters then and later.

Scottish fisherfolk were often cut off socially from the rest of the countryside, which could begin at their garden dyke. Womenfolk never went to sea, but their shore lives were hard, even after they had carried their menfolk to the boats to prevent them from getting their clothes wet! (Not as sexist as it seems – the men would have little chance of drying their clothes once at sea.) Collieston fishwives near Aberdeen walked three miles and back to the Ythan estuary, and then far out at low tide to the mussel scaups to collect fresh bait, several times a week. Once the fish were unloaded it fell to the fishwives to sell them. From the east coast fishing ports, until the early part of the 19th century, women would walk carrying creels, often weighing a hundredweight, up to 30 miles a day to the markets, selling the fish or bartering them for meal and eggs. The *Old Statistical Account* of the 1790s records that the fishwives of Dunbar walked the 27 miles to Edinburgh with 200 pounds of fish in five hours, though that is difficult to credit. From Dunbar inland to Lauder in the Borders runs the 'Herring Road', which was used by the fishwives heading to their rural customers. Those who had the hardest walk were undoubtedly the fishwives of Whaligoe in Caithness. Even before their attempts to sell the fish, they had to climb the cliff from the harbour to the road, carrying their creels, by the 330 steps howked out by the local laird to help the fishing.

The fishwives of the North East coastal ports of Inverallochy, Cairnbulg and Broadsea had things well organised. Christine Watt was born in 1833 and later recalled how she went with her mother to the 'inland country' with cured fish every year through the 1840s and '50s – even selling to the Royal Family at Balmoral. They organised a carter to transport 10 tonnes of fish to a bothy at Corrybeg on upper Deeside, where they lived in primitive conditions, and to which they walked. There they stayed for several weeks, scouring around the Grampians on foot with their creels. Christine recalled that on occasion they would have problems, as local stalking estates tried to block their progress through the glens. Fishwives were fearsome creatures, vituperative and given to swearing, but every account states that their morality was impeccable, and many were religious revivalists. Gradually the walking fishwife disappeared. Scotland's last itinerant fishwife, Betty Millar of Musselburgh, died in 2000. Though she still wore traditional fishwives' garb, her journeys to the Border towns where she sold her fish were made by train.

A change in the organisation of Scottish fishing took place with the herring boom of the 19th century. From half a million, the number of barrels exported rose to a million between 1850 and 1900. In 1880 there were about 40,000 people employed directly in fishing in the season, with another 50,000, mainly women, engaged on the shore side of the industry. The fishquines followed the seasonal migration of the silver darlings down the east coast of Scotland, from Shetland and Wick to the Moray Firth ports, and latterly as far south as Yarmouth in England. Although a much more capitalist industry than was white fishing originally, it took some time before walking was eliminated from the herring. Labour was seasonal, and had to get to the east coast ports from regions of labour surplus, which were mainly in the western Highlands. In the fishing season the population of Wick doubled, with many of the incomers arriving from the west coast – and before railways and other public transport, they walked. Islanders, from Lewis especially, took the ferry to the mainland and joined those from the west of Rosshire and Sutherland, heading mainly for Wick, a walk which took them a week. There the men were busy on the herring boats and the women took employment in the curing. Conditions were terrible. People slept in insanitary bothies, 12 to 15 in each room, the stench in the streets ('putrescent effluvia from fish offal') was indescribable, and typhoid fever was acute and common amongst the workers. Huge amounts of whisky were drunk: as much as 500 gallons a day in the local pubs in Wick. (One minister described them as 'Seminaries of Satan and Belial'.) The Highlanders were not popular, and serious riots erupted between them and the local fishermen in Wick in 1828, to be repeated on a greater scale in 1859 when a three-day riot led to troops being dispatched to the port to restore order.

Though Wick was the most favoured location, many Highlanders walked even further to the Moray coast ports, as this account from 1848 demonstrates:

The fishermen on this eastern coast go out about the middle of July... engaging extra hands, mainly Highlanders, who hire themselves to the owners of the boats for six or eight weeks... Just before the herring boats go out the roads are dotted with little groups of Highlanders, each man having a small parcel of necessaries tied up in a handkerchief and carried on a stick over his shoulder. They are sadly footsore and wayworn by the time they have traversed the island from the west coast [as] the hard roads try them severely. Very little English is spoken amongst them... Wearily and heavily the poor fellows labour along the road [to] Forres, Nairn and the other towns near the shore...

Although this account talks of men, it is clear that the majority who went were women. For example, in 1914, 3,000 women went from Lewis to the herring, and about 1,600 men; a combined total of 20 per cent of the island's population. As the Fishery Officer in Stornoway put it in 1887:

The annual migration from the Lews has been increasing... every man and woman who was without regular employment went [to the herring].

Latterly the Lewis people went by steamer to Kyle, and then by railway to Wick or Aberdeen, whence they took the boat to Shetland – but the railhead did not reach Kyle till 1897, so the tradition of walking to the herring must have continued long after 1848.

The herring industry never fully recovered from the crisis caused by the Great War. The annual migration of fisher-lassies continued, but now by train and steamer. The accounts of the inter-war period show that, though the economic motive was vital in their seasonal migration, these trips were undertaken in part as a working holiday; a female-bonding ritual where they could express themselves more freely than in the regular life of the enclosed, male-dominated, community. That must have been the case for their 19th century predecessors as well.

Fishing was not the only Scottish industry which formerly relied heavily on seasonal labour. Farming, especially at harvest time, could not do without migrant workers, and many of these came surprisingly large distances to and from their employment on foot. Large numbers walked from the impoverished Highlands to the Lowland hairst. Highland harvesters, or shearers, appear regularly in accounts from 1750 onwards, and in 1824 2,500 people turned up to be taken on at the hiring fair at Glasgow Cross. A minister ranted in 1827 about the roads of Argyll being occupied by scores of Highland women returning from the hairst, after spending their wages on fripperies and finery, and having been away from restraining moral influences (of males) all the while. That for the girls it was a holiday, as well as necessary work, is shown by the fact that larger groups often took a piper with them to play on the road, or while they were at work. There was strength in numbers, and often groups of 30, 40 or 50 women, each known to the others, would sign up for the hairst and live together in communal bothies while they laboured. Female labour was favoured because well into the 19th century the harvesting implement was the light-toothed sickle, which women could wield, and their bending ability enabled them to cut the grain to the root.

The Lothian hairst attracted labour from Argyll, but also from much further afield. In 1844 a commentator in Wester Ross wrote of the local girls that 'many went for the harvest. Some as far as the Lothians.' There 46 per cent of the labour force in agriculture was female, higher than elsewhere in Scotland. In the 1880s the Napier Commission on Crofting noted that there was no abatement in the tradition of seasonal migration: 'Many young women went to the Lothians. It is sheer necessity that compels them to go.' While it seems that going to the herring was a long-term pursuit, with many married women involved, the shearers in the Lothians appear to have been mainly in their mid to late teens. Further labour came from an unexpected area – the agricultural North East, where the climate meant the harvest arrived later, and gangs of workers could earn money in the Lothians before working their way back northwards in time for the hairst in the northern lands.

While waiting for the grain to ripen in the cold shoulder of Scotland, many embarked at Aberdeen to sail to Leith for the Lothians. The gangs collected at Aberdeen came from mony airts and pairts, as the following obituary in the *Glasgow Herald* of 1923 indicates:

> The death has taken place at Tiniver, Dufftown, Banffshire of Mr John Gordon who on 2 February celebrated his 99th birthday. A native of the parish of Grange, Banffshire, he entered farm service at an early age, and when a young man would walk to Aberdeen, and proceed by boat to Leith to engage in the Lothian harvests.

Another person who sailed from Aberdeen, after walking there from Deeside, was the young woman who wrote the ballad 'The Lothian Hairst' in the 1860s. Once in Lothian the workers would walk from farm to farm:

> For sax lang weeks the country roon
> Fae toon tae toon we went

The group was under the charge of a foreman (Logan) who, as well as ensuring the lassies worked, had to prevent them engaging in dalliances with the local lads, clearly much to the regret of the sangstress:

> My mate and I could get nae chance
> For Logan's watchfu eye
> And wi the lads we got nae sport
> For Logan was sae sly

The independence and adventure of the hairst clearly counted with the lassies almost as much as their pay of about £1 a week at harvest time, and songs abound of the association of the hairst with romance and courting. It would not appear from these songs that the female shearers shared the strict moral code of the fisherquines. While the latter would sing of their hope that their anchor would hold in the storms of life, the former were more likely to express a wish that a ploughboy might wrap them in his plaidie. But with men like Logan policing the living quarters, they had little chance.

The shearers lived in farm outbuildings in some cases, but as time passed bothies were specially constructed for them. They normally had no running water and no toilet, though a fire and coals were usually provided. Some had stone floors, some had earthen. Though living conditions were generally poor, the hairst workers, unlike general farm labourers outside hairst time, appear to have been well fed, with porridge, milk, bread, beer and meat provided by the farmer in addition to their wages.

North East harvesters moved from farm to farm in the Lothians, and then worked the harvest on foot northwards towards Stirling, the Carse of Gowrie, Fife, or even to the west of Scotland where the hairst came later than in the Lothians. Some would make their own way back to the North East, and it was probably one such group that Queen

Victoria saw when she was crossing the old drove road from Deeside to Fettercairn in 1860, over the shoulder of Mount Keen. This route would have been the most direct back from central Scotland for seasonal workers from Upper Deeside. Victoria encountered the group resting prior to their crossing of the mountain, at the foot of the Ladder Burn:

> We crossed the burn at the bottom where a pictur-esque group of 'shearers' were seated, chiefly women, the older ones smoking. They were returning from the south to the north, whence they came.

The fact that some of the women were smoking must have appalled Victoria, who detested the habit. A common concern amongst contemporary commentators is the loss of social and sexual control over mobile women earning wages.

The introduction of Irish male labour, with the scythe-heuk, contributed to the decline of female shearing. The scythe could cut more and faster than the sickle, although not so well, and male labour was more expensive. So there was still a demand for seasonal female labour in the Lothians in 1900. However, with other opportunities opening up for women, they were gradually voting with their feet and abandoning farm labour, despite the increased wages which were being offered. Though many still trudged between farms for the hairst, few, if any, actually walked to the Lothians, given the spread of the railway system by this time. The bands of shearers and fisher lassies, groups of women laughing and singing as they escaped for a few weeks to earn their tocher and have some fun, had left the roads.

Suggested Walks

WALK 19

The Herring Road, Longformacus to Lauder (OS 67 and 73)

The earlier part of the Herring Road from Dunbar is difficult and unrewarding to follow. But this walk covers a good section of the latter part of the route of the fishwives' journey, and is part of the waymarked Southern Upland Way.

From Longformarcus a good road goes to the Watch Water reservoir, and continues over rougher ground, climbing westward to the Twin Law Cairns (possibility of shelter here), and then Rutherford's Cairn, before descending over Nun Rig to Braidshawrig. Then the route goes down Scoured Rig and crosses the Snawdon Burn before arriving at Lauder.

Longformacus to Lauder: 14 miles, 7 hours.

WALK 20

The Firmounth Road (OS 44)

This was one of the main routes taken by itinerant harvesters from the North East to the earlier hairsts in the Lothians and Strathmore. It was an old whisky road, and also a drove road. A Right of Way case in the 1930s prevented the route being closed by the Coats family (of Paisley cotton fame) who owned Glentanar at that time. The judge in the case noted the evidence brought to him of 'a considerable body of travelling farms hands going south top the harvesting and shearing' by the route in the 19th century.

From Glentanar House, cross the bridge and take the left fork alongside a plantation (marked Firmounth Road on the OS map). This climbs to the east of Craigmahandle and then crosses the shoulder of Gannoch (731 m) by St Colm's Well, which is marked by a memorial. In medieval times this was a pilgrimage point on the saint's feast day, 16 October. A little further on is a cairn marked WE 1814, where a tinker is reputed to have murdered his wife. After crossing Tampie, the route descends and joins the Fungle Road before dropping easily to Shinfur and Tarfside. An alternative is to take the Fungle back north to Aboyne, about 4 miles from Glentanar House, making a circular walk which simplifies transport logistics.

Glen Tanar to Tarfside: 11 miles, 5–6 hours.

CHAPTER II

Irish Itinerants

IRISH MONKS SUCH AS Columba had walked through Scotland in the missionary years of Christianity. Much later a large proportion of the Marquis of Montrose's Royalist forces in the Covenanting wars, especially in the year of his amazing victories over the armies of the Scottish Parliament in 1645, had been Irishmen on foot. They covered some distance: Kilsyth, Dundee, Aberdeen (which they sacked, slaughtering many inhabitants), Alford, Elgin and Auldearn all saw the largely foot-army. Their progress was recorded in a North East ballad, 'The Bonnie Lass o' Fyvie':

> There once was a troop o' Irish dragoons
> Cam marchin doon through Fyvie-o
> And the captain's fa'en in love wi a very bonny lass
> And her name it is ca'ed pretty Peggy-o

Montrose's Irishmen crossed the mountains of Lochaber via Loch Treig, where their hair froze to their heads. They also partly traversed the Corrieyairack Pass to surprise and defeat the Campbells at Inverlochy, subsequently disgracing themselves with a terrible slaughter of civilians in Argyll. Finally they were routed and themselves massacred by David Leslie's forces at Philiphaugh, near Selkirk.

The passage of time brought more peaceful Irish itinerants to Scotland's shores. Many of these were to leave a lasting mark, through their work in constructing roads, railways and dams, and from their eventual permanent residence in the country. Large numbers of Ulstermen came to Scotland for their higher education, and when industrialisation began the relatively skilled and educated Scots-Irish found little difficulty in crossing to the old country and finding good employment. But for the overwhelmingly Catholic population of Donegal, things were different. Poor and ill-educated, they tended to slot into Scottish society at the lowest level, and from the famine years of the 1840s Irish immigration into Scotland became overwhelmingly Catholic.

Initially many Irish saw Scotland as a source of seasonal labour. But each wave tended to leave its residue behind. By 1900 the Irish-born constituted 15 per cent of Glasgow's population. In the 1820s, 6–8,000 Irish were coming over each year for the seasonal harvest work, carrying their scythes wrapped in straw. This number increased to 40,000 in the famine years, but declined back to about 4,000 a year by the 1880s. They landed on the west coast and walked eastwards, starting work in the Lothians and working their way back to the west and the boat to Ireland. Unlike the Scottish migrant harvesters, the Irish were (mostly) men, possibly a reflection of the social conservatism of Catholic Ireland, and perhaps also because the Irish harvested with the scythe, an instrument supposedly too heavy for women to work with.

Conditions for the Irish workers on the crossing to Scotland were appalling. In 1848 the *Londonderry* arrived in Glasgow with 72 dead passengers in its hold, and even 60 years later the four-shilling crossing from Donegal entitled the ticket holder to a passage next to defecating cattle. Thankfully the crossing was short. The Irish shearers appear to have experienced working and living conditions not markedly different from the Scots they laboured with, apart from being better paid. As they were male, and could cut 50 per cent faster than the sickle-wielding women, their wages reflected this. Accounts speak of little hostility between Irish and Scots shearers, but little mixing either; sexual and religious differences probably accounted for this. One female farm worker recalled that in the period 1900–14, the same group of half a dozen Irish male shearers, the Doyles, came each year to the farm where she was a servant in East Lothian. They lived in a bothy with no water or sanitation, and stood aloof from the Farm Servants Union, fearing for their re-employment. Even on rest days they did not mix, walking miles to the nearest Catholic chapel and back.

Despite the spread of mechanical reaping, the demand for seasonal labour on Scottish farms continued. There was much work in the weeding, tattie howking and berry picking to be done. Many groups contributed to this labour – travelling people and miners' wives as well as the Irish labourers. These agricultural activities appear to have been more sexually mixed than shearing, and accounts describe gangs of male and female labour. In Robert McLellan's lovely story 'The Donegals', set on a Lanarkshire fruit farm before the Great War, the Irish labourers are mixed sex:

> The mairrit anes had the auld bothy abune the milk-hoose... but the single weemen bade at the tae end o' the big barn, and the single men at the tither, wi a raw o' auld blankets hung up for a waa atween them... whan the Donegals were aa beddit doun at nicht... my grandfather lockit the muckle yett at the closs mou.

This locking in of the seasonal labourers at night was traditional, and continued until a dreadful fire in Kirkintilloch in 1937, in which 10 people died. When the fruit picking was over the Donegals set off 'to the upland ferms for the hey and the tatties', according to McLellan.

The traditional male dominance amongst Irish migrant workers was never challenged in areas where their unskilled labour was at a premium. The large-scale construction sites, such as the canals and railways, attracted massive inflows of Irish labour, the 'navvies', and in the days before motorised transport groups of men would walk from a completed project to another about to begin.

The Irish migrant labourer was untroubled by craft consciousness and demarcation lines; he would do any work available, and there was a cross-over between those who worked on construction projects and those who did unskilled agricultural labour. This can be seen in Patrick MacGill's autobiographical *Children of the Dead End*, in which he features as Dermod Flynn. MacGill spent a decade in Scotland before 1914 as a navvy, and his narrative is valuable as so few accounts of their own labour written by working people exist, and it must describe the mute experience of many thousands of his compatriots walking through Scotland.

MacGill was born in Donegal. At the age of 12 his family needed money for their rent and taxes to the Church, and he was sent 'beyond the mountains' to walk with other barefoot children, carrying their shoes, to the railway and a train which would take them all to a hiring market in Strabane. Two years of work later, he took the Derry boat to Scotland. MacGill describes the crossing:

> They were all very ragged, both women and men; most of the men were drunk, and they discussed, quarrelled, argued and swore till the din was deafening... All over the deck and down in the steerage the harvestmen and

labourers fought one another for hours on end. Over the bodies of the women who were asleep, over coils of ropes, trunks and boxes of clothes, the drunken men struggled like demons... until the drink and exertion overpowered them at last.

MacGill initially worked picking potatoes. One bothy he stayed in was a pigsty overrun with rats, which the men killed, earning a halfpenny a tail from the farmer. They raked in £3 – that's 1,500 rats. The men lifted the tatties with graips; the women followed on their knees, putting them in baskets. Hours were long and there were no bad-weather breaks. They walked from farm to farm throughout the howking season; when that ended, MacGill was on the tramp and headed for Glasgow.

For several years MacGill roamed west central Scotland. At times he collected scrap metal; at other times he lived by poaching. Sometimes he slept out of doors, and other times in the various model lodging houses which were home for the Irish navvies. At the lodging house in Greenock he met his old friend Moleskin Joe, who told him of the work with good pay to be had at a huge construction project deep in the Highlands. They decided to head off north the next day for the promised land of Kinlochleven, with little but the tattered clothes and worn boots they stood up in. A tin of matches, a pipe and a knife were all they carried, with a metal can for drinking and cooking.

The distance from Greenock to Kinlochleven is almost 100 miles and the men took six days to walk it, at a rate of over 15 miles a day. They could have gone faster, but part of the attraction of the tramp was its pleasure, and they took their time. 'The pace of the road is not a sharp one', MacGill says, '"Slow and easy goes far in a day" is a saying amongst us.' Joe and MacGill, lacking the ferry fare, stole a boat and rowed across the Clyde, continuing their tramp and begging, until they were well past Dumbarton and on the Loch Lomond road. Thereabouts they lit a fire and ate their meal, the *chef d'oeuvre* being a hen which Moleskin had tempted onto the king's highway and killed there (the location of the crime apparently mitigating its seriousness, in his eyes at least).

As they came to the less populated countryside, problems emerged. The weather turned – 'it rained and rained', says MacGill, and there were few places to beg or even shelter. After crossing Rannoch Moor, they came to 'the Kings Arms' (the Kingshouse Hotel), starving. Moleskin managed to liberate a rooster from the hen house there, but it escaped and began to crow, rousing the hotelier. Joe threw a boot at the bird and missed, but eventually MacGill strangled it and the pair ran away from the bird's owner over the moor, with Moleskin hopping in one boot. As they cooked their ill-gotten gains, MacGill gave his pair of boots to Moleskin and walked the last day's journey to Kinlochleven barefoot. The next day the pair crossed the hills, probably by the Allt Lagan na Feithe, and arrived at what MacGill called 'the Mecca of our hopes'. He describes the scene he saw from the watershed:

> A sleepy hollow lay below; and within it a muddle of shacks, roofed with tarred canvas, and built of driven piles, were huddled together in bewildering confusion. These were surrounded by puddles, heaps of disused wood, tins, bottles and all manner of discarded rubbish. Some of the shacks had windows, most of them had none... it looked as if the buildings had fallen from the sky by accident...

Inside these one-roomed shacks thousands of men lived, cooked, slept, gambled and fought their way through the construction of the Blackwater Dam. Fifty bunks to a shack, a dirt floor and no sanitation – that was the lot of the men who lived there (a few Highlanders and some Poles, but mainly the Irish). Some of them died at the site of the dam. The work of blasting and quarrying was very dangerous, and in the graveyard below, not far from the rubbish dump, many are recalled only by their nicknames on the flaking tombstones, while many others are simply 'Not Known'. Others died crossing the pass in winter towards the public bar of the Kingshouse Hotel, and their bodies were discovered in the spring. The only time the law came to the camp was in the form of two armed policemen who accompanied the postman bringing letters from Ireland. Despite the predominance of Irish labourers, no Catholic priest came to Kinlochleven, and the navvies appear to have lost their contacts with religion, unlike the shearers mentioned earlier. MacGill himself had renounced religion after listening to socialist public speakers in Glasgow.

When the job was over they left the Blackwater behind. Many headed southwards to Glasgow, others eastwards to the new naval base being built at Rosyth in Fife. In a moving passage MacGill describes this Great Exodus:

> The great procession filed down the hillside. Hundreds of men had been paid off the same evening... We were an army of scarecrows, ragged unkempt scarecrows of civilisation. Some were old, lame men who might not live until they obtained their next job. They had built their last town. Strong lusty fellows like myself took the lead...
>
> Some sang as they journeyed along. They sang

about love, and drink, about women and gambling...
Suddenly the sound of singing died... A great silence
fell on the party. The nailed shoes rasping on the hard
earth... were the only sounds that could be heard in
the darkness.

And down the face of the mountain the ragged
army tramped slowly on.

The tradition of Irish seasonal labourers coming to Scotland
continued in the inter-war years, though with the economic
recession there were fewer opportunities for work and the
former mass movement eased. Nevertheless, in agriculture and
construction work the brogue of the Irish navvy only disappeared slowly from Scotland. Many Irish labourers crossed
to work in the building of the hydro-dams in the 1950s, for
example. Indeed, even today the lilt can occasionally be
heard at some construction sites as an unexpected relic of
the past. After the Great War, seasonal and casual labour
was carried around the country by motor transport, and the
days had gone when the roads were full of navvies walking
to and from construction sites like the Blackwater Dam.

Moleskin Joe used to say, 'There's a good time comin,'
though we may never live to see it.' From the 1950s the
gradual assimilation of Irish immigrants into Scottish society
gathered pace, but for Joe and thousands of others that good
time never came. Nor did it come for those unemployed
Glasgow workers in the 1930s who, hearing of an expansion
of the aluminium works at Kinlochleven, followed in the
tracks of Moleskin 30 years later. Neil Munro watched them
with astonishment and horror from the comfort of his railway
carriage, the broken men on another kind of hunger march:

There is no hour of the day, and no part of the road

on which they are not to be witnessed... the rejected of Commerce, for whom the great new works at Kinlochleven... proffer a chance in a thousand that there may be work and pay... sight to startle, grieve, alarm... Ah! comrades, beaten comrades, far is the cry to Polmadie!

Men like these, and Moleskin before, tramped the virtual route of the present-day West Highland Way with empty bellies and holes in their boots, from a necessity born of poverty.

Suggested Walks

WALK 21

Altnafeadh to the Blackwater Dam (OS 41)

It is uncertain the exact route Molsekin Joe and the others would have taken from Glencoe to their camp at the Blackwater, so this circular route covers both possibilities. The first section also encompasses a section of the old military road to Fort William, now part of the West Highland Way.

Ascend the intimidating sounding but very easy Devil's Staircase to the col and then descend until the route of the West Highland Way is joined from the right by a Land Rover track, and take this track east until the Blackwater Dam is reached. This still provides hydro-electricity, but not any longer for the closed Kinlochleven smelter.

The navvy village is easy to locate by the mounds of rubbish around its site, and also from the location of the graveyard by the burn just below the dam. Return to Glencoe by Warbrick's Loch and the Allt Lagan na Feithe and Lochan na Feithe to Altnafeadh. This latter was probably the navvies' route, shorter despite being rougher, and this was the way the overhead pully-system carried supplies to the dam. The navvies took this route to the pub at Kingshouse, and MacGill states that some died on the way back of exposure.

Round trip: 11 miles, 6 hours.

WALK 22

Broomielaw to Lanark by the Clyde Walkway (os 64 and 72)

Irish itinerant shearers and fruit pickers would have landed by ship at the Broomielaw, and walked to their workplaces. Whilst the route of the present Clyde Walkway does not exactly follow the route the fruit pickers would have taken to the farms, it gives a good idea of the countryside they travelled through. It is the longest walk in this book and one of the best, laden down with historical references, though how many of these the Irish farm labourers would have taken cognisance of is open to conjecture. The walk takes three full days, but you could spend a week on it. Most of it is reasonably well maintained and quite well signposted: one or two locations require a bit of gumption.

If you walk the full length of the Broomielaw you experience Glasgow's changing waterfront to its best, before entering Glasgow Green, just after passing 'Paddy's Market', a set of stalls originally vending clothes etc to the Irish poor, but now inter-denominational. On Glasgow Green the People's Palace Museum commemorates the working class history of the city, and contains information on the Irish contribution. Thereafter you take the path along the bends of the Clyde, where you seem a hundred miles from Glasgow, until you leave the city and cross the Clyde 'half a mile afore Carmyle' by the Cambuslang Bridge into Lanarkshire. Then you pass (after crossing the Clyde again) Uddingston, beyond where

Bothwell Castle is one of Scotland's finest and then Blantyre where the NTS runs the David Livingstone Centre on the site of the mill the missionary worked in as a child (reached by a bridge across the Clyde). At Bothwell is the site of the Battle of Bothwell Brig, scene of the defeat of the Covenanters in 1679, and then in Strathclyde Country Park there is an opportunity to visit the fine Roman bath house at Bothwellhaugh, relocated from its initial site when the artificial loch was created. The main attraction is the Baron's Haugh RSPB bird sanctuary, and beyond this you leave post-industrial Lanarkshire behind, and enter post-agricultural Lanarkshire.

At Dalserf, a lovely wee village with a delightful church, you enter the once fruit-growing lands of Clydesdale, which have recently been experiencing a revival in their economic fortunes, as the former glasshouses become garden centres. Where once Irish immigrants cleared the trees of their fruit, Polish immigrants now clear the tables in the coffee shops. The route continues for a couple of miles on the A712 up the west side of the river as far as Crossford, where it crosses to the east side and continues past Strathbyres Linn to Kirkfieldbank. You can here cross the Clydesholm Bridge (dating from the 1690s) and proceed direct to New Lanark, but a fitting climax to this walk to continue on the west bank of the Clyde to Bonnington Linn, crossing the river here and then walking back down the east bank of the Clyde to New Lanark, the UNESCO World Heritage Site celebrating the socialist and co-operative ideas of Robert Owen. From here it is a steep climb up the brae to Lanark. Lanark itself is rich in William Wallace and Covenanter associations, and here you can get the train back to Glasgow.

Glasgow to New Lanark by the route described to

Bonnington Linn, 43 miles; to Lanark, 45 miles. It takes at least three days to do this walk (given the time consuming attractions en route) preferably five to cover all the side trips, and accommodation can easily be found anywhere along the route (Youth Hostel and hotel at New Lanark). Or accessible trains can take you back to Glasgow nightly. Take Ian Lees' *On Foot through Clydesdale* (1932), if you can find a copy.

CHAPTER 12

Walking in and out of Town

FROM EARLY TIMES in Scottish towns the middle classes took the air, displaying their fine clothing and socialising. The reservation of the 'croon o' the causey' for the superior orders in many burghs – to keep them dry-shod while the lower orders used the gutters – reflects this. In the 18th and 19th centuries, new middle class districts reached out from the urban slums, and these were provided with public parks or private gardens for constitutionals. The walking in these parks would have been indulged in for display and supervised courtship, rather than for exercise per se.

In 1848 *An Address to the Middle Classes on the Subject of Gymnastic Exercises* was published. It pointed out that, while the aristocracy went a-hunting and the working classes laboured, the middle classes were becoming sedentary, using cabs and eating too much. The working classes certainly laboured, and were fortunate in not being able to over-eat or afford cabs, and they continued to do a surprising amount of urban walking. The St Andrew's Suspension Bridge was built at Glasgow Green in 1856, specifically to allow factory workers pedestrian access over the River Clyde to their employment, and walking to work is one of the unwritten aspects of urban life. Here we can only give a few examples of walking in (and out of) town.

Many migrants to the growing urban areas arrived on foot. Before railways, Highland migrants to Glasgow walked. The mother of John MacLean (the famous Clydeside socialist) was a victim of the Highland famine in the 1840s, and walked with her own mother to Paisley from Corpach near Fort William. MacLean himself was no mean walker, and while a student at the Free Kirk Training College on the north side of the city he walked daily there and back from Pollokshaws, at least 50 miles a week. The Highland community represented five per cent of Glasgow's population of one million in around the year 1900 and was the largest ethnic group after the Irish. The Highlanders developed their own, semi-institutional forms of urban walking.

There is a marvellous piece of Victorian engineering, in riveted cast-iron and glass, which carries the railway from Glasgow Central over Argyle Street. Recently restored to its original glory, it boasts a plaque denoting its name: the 'Hielanman's Umbrella'. The name comes from the habit of the Glasgow Gaels of meeting there, often using the bridge as a shelter from the inclement weather. Glasgow's Gaels predominantly worked in domestic service in areas like Park Circus, and in the industries to the north and south of the navigable stretch of the Clyde, for example in the bustling river ferries, known as the 'Skye Navy'. Most also lived in the riparian areas of Govan, Kinning Park and Partick. The Umbrella was convenient for this riverside littoral.

Arriving in the city in the era of horse-drawn omnibuses and later trams, the Highlander appears only slowly to have given up the willingness to walk. The servant girls of the Park area would meet on their half-day off, and walk (safety in numbers) along the Great Western Road to the Botanic Gardens or further. Walking to church was also a Highland tradition, as using other transport was seen as breaking strict sabbatarian rules. In Glasgow this tradition continued into the 1950s, when Gaels from the South Side walked to kirks across the river.

People would meet at the Umbrella between services, for example walking down from St Columba's Gaelic Church of Scotland to the 'Hielanman's', and swapping news from the homelands and of urban events. If the weather was fine, various groups would depart from the Umbrella in an urban promenade, in several directions, returning to exchange more gossip. As well as its Sabbath function, the Umbrella was used as a weekend and evening meeting place, and doubtless many a troth was plighted beneath its girders as couples 'walked out' together (a phrase showing the traditional link between courtship and walking).

At its height in the 1920s and '30s, the Umbrella tradition did not survive the social disruption of World War II and the blackout, and soon became a fond memory. The educationally successful and upwardly mobile Gael moved away from the banks of the Clyde, and the greatest concentration of Kelvinside Krofters is now in middle class Milngavie, where the 'Street' is a source of imaginary suburban terrors.

A similar form of urban *paseo* took place in Aberdeen. Youth culture tends to be associated with the 1960s, but between the wars 'Tally' cafés, dance halls and cinemas gave the urban youth a freedom which their parents, who had grown up in a pre-1914 (adult) culture of pubs and music halls, had lacked. However, it was the Depression and entertainment had to be cheaply found. Everything (the pubs and cafés) closed early in those days, so when 'the picters' came out, the teenagers of Aberdeen 'wakked the matt'. Many of the cinemas were located on Union Street and groups of youths of both sexes would promenade up and down the south side, engaging in courtship rituals. This performance was repeated – hence the reference to wearing out the mat – and attempts were made to get a lumber before the last buses and trams.

The shoes chosen for this form of walking were probably not of the sensible kind.

The successful 'coorters' might meet the next day at the 'Monkey Hoose' on the Union Street/Union Terrace junction, where shelter was offered against the weather in a bank's portico. Those who had been unsuccessful would 'wakk the matt' again on the Sunday, hopefully to join the lucky coupled pairs who were heading for an ice cream parlour or the carnivals at the beach esplanade, and windy romance. Unlike the Glasgow Highlanders whose *paseo* was for all ages, 'wakkin the matt' was for the 16 to 20-ish age group. As with the Umbrella, the disruption of the War and changing post-war social patterns dealt severe blows to the event. But, even in the swinging sixties, it was not unknown for groups of youths to wander Union Street on a Sunday, past closed shops, pubs and cafés, hoping their sexual luck might turn.

At the same time as the Highlanders were walking in Glasgow, others were walking out of it. The 1920s and '30s were times of social explosion. As cafés and cinemas revolutionised social life, so organisations like the Youth Hostels opened up the countryside for urban dwellers. Many working class people participated in these movements, but not everything was provided for them – quite remarkable efforts were made, often by people in difficult circumstances, to forge their own social landscapes. Walking played its part in this.

After World War I, a landowner outside Glasgow allowed an ex-serviceman to build a holiday shack, a sort of dacha, on his land at Carbeth, about 10 miles north of the city. Soon a village of very similar huts, with bitumen roofs and green timber walls, sprouted throughout the forest landscape. Hutters paid a nominal rent and facilities were installed at the residents' own expense. The place became a veritable holiday camp, and a burn was dammed to make an outdoor swimming pool in this co-operative version of a Butlins. Many of the hutters came from the west side of Glasgow (places like Scotstoun), and especially from Clydebank just outside the city boundaries. And many of them walked to Carbeth to spend the weekends or summer holidays there. The suburban railway ended at Milngavie and, in pre-car days, those coming from Glasgow had to travel on foot a distance of about four miles from the station. They approached the huts through a defile which they called, with typical Clydeside humour, 'the Khyber Pass'.

But the Bankies coming to Carbeth had a bigger problem: to get to Milngavie meant going into Glasgow first. This was time consuming and expensive, so many simply walked over the Kilpatrick Hills from Clydebank, past Craigton, to Carbeth – a much shorter route. Those lucky enough to have a dacha also profited when the Blitz hit Clydebank in 1941 and housing provision for the displaced was a problem. In some cases local families decamped to Carbeth, again crossing the Kilpatricks, where many of them had initially fled to escape the German bombers. I was amazed to find that some Bankies walk this route to the huts even now.

Carbeth also played a role in getting the urban working class adventurer out onto the Highland hills. Many of the early Clydeside mountaineers were victims of the Depression. The climbers met at Craigallion Loch, a little south of the Carbeth huts, where a fire was reputedly never allowed to go out, such was the coming and going of walkers, mountaineers and tramps. From Craigallion they pushed further northwards to the Campsies, along the water pipeline track to Loch Katrine and westwards to Ben Arthur ('the Cobbler', near Loch Lomond), occasionally hitch-hiking but largely on foot.

Ian Thompson's biography of the Clydeside socialist mountaineer *Jock Nimlin* gives details from Nimlin's diaries of when he was unemployed. They show that Nimlin was as welcome at the huts of Carbeth as he was at the Craigallion fire, and would walk or hitch out from Glasgow, using Carbeth as a base, to undertake massive walking expeditions into the Highlands. He would often engage in casual labour on farms and estates there before dropping back to the fire at the lochside, or to the hut of a friend at the suburban staging post. 'Slept at Carbeth' and 'Home by Craigallion' are frequent entries in Nimlin's diaries.

The future of the unique settlement at Carbeth is sadly now uncertain due to increased rents and a lack of facilities, a tense issue for the hutters who still enjoy this prime location outside Glasgow. The old swimming pool is silted up and grown over with reeds; but contrary to what Thomson says in *Jock Nimlin*, Craigallion Loch is still very much there, and indeed is passed by tens of thousands of people doing the West Highland Way. Hopefully they might give a thought to these tatty but cosy huts which for a previous generation were the springboard to an 'Undiscovered Scotland'.

Walking out of town to places like Carbeth was one response of unemployed workers to their situation in the 1930s. Another was to take part in political activity, especially hunger marches, and many hundreds of politicised Clydeside workers did so. However, the longest of the marches was that faced by the contingent from Aberdeen. Their feat of endurance in walking over 600 miles on the way to London in 1936 was officially recognised by having the Granite City contingent lead the assembled marchers from all over the country into the capital. There were many such marches in the 1930s, some of them backed by the official Labour Party and Trade

Unions. Others, however, like the 1936 Aberdeen march, were organised by the National Unemployed Workers' Movement. These communist-organised marches were officially shunned. Official marchers got capes, groundsheets and boots, and their accommodation was organised en route, but the unofficial marchers had to re-learn the skills of Moleskin Joe.

Behind a banner reading 'Aberdeen to London. United against the Means Test', three dozen marchers, including lone representatives from Inverness and Peterhead, had set out on 26 September. Apart from personal items their only comfort was 15 blankets donated by the workers at Grandholm Mills. Thousands of supporters gathered in the Gallowgate and many marched with the men to the Brig o' Dee and the edge of the city. One marcher, John Lennox, recalls:

> We jist wore fit we had, wer ordinary clais... some o' them had a bit o' an auld raincoat, probably from a jumble sale... They were willin but, oh there wis fellas physically caved in after years o' unemployment. They had never been nourished... but the majority o' them made it to London.

The marchers took four days to get to Dundee, at between 15 and 20 miles a day. Their first night's stop was at Stonehaven, where they were forced to sleep on the floor in a harbour hut. At Dundee the reception was enthusiastic, with a huge crowd, and they proceeded through the Fife mining districts where a warm reception was also encountered. This was a contrast with Edinburgh: 'Oh, thon was the worst of all the places we were in! It was a Tory dominated place and it was a cold, cold reception we got...'

By now the marchers had recruited to about 200 and this posed problems with supplies on the next section of the march, through the sparsely populated and politically unsympathetic Scottish Borders and rural northern England. Their route took them through Galashiels, Hawick, Langholm, Carlisle, Alston, Middleton in Teesdale, Barnard Castle, Richmond ('that was a real Tory place, Richmond') and Harrogate.

> We were really hungry. As a matter o' fact we had tae send oot an appeal to the country. Supplies run oot a'thegither. We were the best part o' seven or eight days on that particular route.
>
> Jock Winton was an official collector. You would see a farm hoose... a mile there and a mile back. And Jock would come back wi a bloody hen. Now he swore blind that he was given it. He never come back empty handed...

One bright spark on this bleak section was crossing the border. Normally the banner was furled except when passing through towns, but the marchers allowed themselves a gesture: 'Bein Scots they made the maist o' the actual crossing – a conquering army come across wi the banners wavin!' Music was provided by a kazoo band, and later by Fife miners on the pipes. Things improved in Leeds where they were re-clothed: 'The boys were a' getting new troosers – after all, their boots and clais wis, well, they were sleepin in them, walking in them.' A great boost was given when the east coast contingent joined up with the Scottish west coast marchers at St Albans and entered London a thousand strong.

Just as many working people gained a sense of purpose through their discovery of walking in the outdoors in the 1930s, so many more gained self-respect and an antidote to despair in political activity such as the hunger marches.

The hunger march was one o' the highlights of my life,

WALKING IN AND OUT OF TOWN

really. There was conviction behind it, ye see. There was real purpose, we did gain, there was a change in the means test and there was concessions the Government did make as a result o' the march.

Suggested Walks

WALK 23

The Highlanders' Trail (Any Glasgow Street Atlas)

Start at the Hielanman's Umbrella under Central Station on Argyle Street, where a plaque on the north side of the street commemorates the name, but fails to explain the social significance of this meeting place and urban-walking launch-pad. Go up Hope Street and then along Waterloo Street, and at its end turn up Pitt Street to St Vincent Street. Here are two churches long associated with Glasgow's Highland community. The Church of Scotland's St Columba's Church on St Vincent Street itself is one of the last still to hold Gaelic services, whilst the world famous Greek Thomson church on the corner with Pitt Street served many from the Free Kirk congregations.

Elmbank Street and Bath Street take you across the motorway to Berkeley Street. Just opposite the Mitchell Library is a block of new flats on Berkeley Street. Here for many years was the Highlanders' Institute, where the many and various Gaelic organisations in the city held their social events.

Further along Berkeley Street, Elderslie Street leads you north into the Park district. On Lynedoch Street are the three towers of the magnificent Trinity Church which was for many years also the seminary for Free Kirk ministers and teachers. John MacLean, the great Glasgow socialist, initially studied here, walking a 10 mile round trip from Pollokshaws, his home. There were many Highgland servant lassies in the Park area, and on their half day off they would wander into Kelvingrove Park, and then walk up Great Western Road. A little to the right of the bridge over the River Kelvin lies a stone marked D.D. An Clachan 1911. This marks the spot where a Highland village was created at the Empire Exhibition that year to illustrate the life of the Highlander as one of the tribes of the Empire. If you take the Gray Street exit from the park and continue on down to Argyle Street you will come to the Park Bar, where you are more likely to hear Gaelic spoken than anywhere else on the Scottish mainland.

Hielanman's Umbrella to the Park Bar: c. 4 miles, 2 hours.

WALK 24

The Bankies Trek (OS 64, and any Glasgow Street Atlas)

Take the train from Glasgow to either Clydebank or Kilbowie stations, then either walk up Kilbowie Road till its very end, and continue up Faifley Road, or take the bus to the Faifley terminus. The Bankies who fled the Blitz had to do the whole route, often pushing prams laden with their kids and possessions.

From the bus terminus a path, marked on the OS map, goes uphill through wood and moorland, and then joins a farm track which descends to Tambowie. From the high point, where many Bankies spent nights in the open avoiding the bombing, the view of the Clyde and Glasgow is impressive. From Tambowie, a half mile walk north on the A809 is necessary, and then another half mile east on an unclassified road, till the route of the West Highland Way is attained. This goes north past Craigallion Loch, meeting place of the

Creag Dhu climbers in the 1930s, and then through the Khyber Pass to the Carbeth huts. The views north to the Campsies are fine. From Carbeth take the West Highland Way back the way you initially came, and then continue down through the delightful Mugdock Wood to Milngavie, and get the train back to Glasgow.

From Faifley to Carbeth, and then back to Milngavie: 9 miles, 4 hours.

CHAPTER 13

Tinkers' Loan

THOSE WHO WALKED THROUGH Scottish history over the last 2,000 years did so largely because they were obliged to in order to earn their living or engage in battle, or to save their souls. They may have enjoyed their walking – the evidence is that many did. But to be on the road was a means to an end, not the end in itself.

However, there have always been an awkward minority for whom the medium was the message – people who tramped the highways and byways for pure pleasure and through a dislike of urban life or settled labour, or both. Beggars, tramps, hawkers, gypsies and tinkers have been on the roads of Scotland for as long as the roads have been there. In the Catholic period, mendicant monks travelled the roads receiving alms, and to give money to a beggar was seen as one of the 'good works' leading to salvation. The Protestant work ethic put a stop to such attitudes and begging became frowned upon. An exception was that of the king's licensed beggars, who were given tokens of eligibility, and of whom Edie Ochiltree in Scott's novel *The Antiquary* is an example. Social change increased displaced persons and vagrancy, and the victims were not looked upon with sympathy. In the early 18th century, noting that beggars were pestering and threatening honest folk, and stealing forbye, Andrew Fletcher of Saltoun proposed that vagrants be forced into slave labour for the common good. Many laws were already in the Statute Book concerning vagabonds and providing for their punishment – including, in

1665, one advocating the transportation 'of strong and idle beggars, Gypsies and criminals to Jamaica'.

By general consensus, such vagrants were idle wretches who scorned any opportunity to work and deserved little sympathy. While it may be politically incorrect to say so, various traditional Scottish songs of the road about the life of vagrants and tramps would appear to agree with this:

> O' aa the trades that I dae ken
> The beggin is the best
> For when a beggar man gets tired
> He can lay him doon tae rest.
>
> And some will gie me beef and bried
> And some will gie me cheese
> And I'll be oot amang the fowk
> A pickin-up bawbees.

Many songs about tramping speak with joy about the life, and the beauty of the countryside, and express little sorrow at being excluded from the world of work:

> I'm happy in the simmer-time
> Aneath the bricht blue sky
> Nae thinkin in the mornin
> At nicht far I'm tae lie
> Barns or byres or onyroads
> Or oot amang the hey
> And if the weather daes permit
> I am happy everyday.

The author of this latter song, 'Come aa ye Tramps and Hawker Lads', records in verse that he has travelled far and wide in Scotland – he's been in bonny Gallowa' and doon aboot Stranraer, Loch Katrine and Loch Lomond have been seen by his eyes and 'the Dee, the Don and the Deveron, that hurries intae the sea' are also familiar to him, all visited on feet 'weary and blistered'. The social origins of the tramps must have been very varied, though many were probably casualties of urban economic life. In the 1930s we saw that Jock Nimlin briefly became a tramp, and many other single men found that life on the road was easier than that in the unemployment-infested cities of the time. However these tramps, hawkers and vagabonds should not be confused with Scotland's traditional travelling people, the tinkers. The latter were organised social groups rather than isolated individuals and had a vital economic role to play in the countryside. As one Sutherland traveller said, not unkindly, of an Irish tramp: 'Charlie Doyle just lives frae day tae day – but we live entirely in the past.'

'Tinker' or 'tinkler' simply means tinsmith, which many of the original travellers were. This name has negative connotations in the epithet 'tink', and the term 'travelling people' is now preferred. The origins of Scotland's travellers is obscure, but one thing is certain – they are not gypsies in any sense, the latter being a distinct ethnic group of possible Hindi origin (although gypsies have been known in Scotland since the Middle Ages). Gypsies were also less tolerated than tinkers because the former were less likely to work, living by their musical talents and fortune-telling, as well as by sorning (begging) and stealing. The tinkers, whatever they are, are native Scots; those in the Highlands talking Gaelic (with various admixtures) and the Lowland ones braid Scots (again with Gaelic and Romany words). In rural Scotland, both Highland and Lowland, their traditional role as tinsmiths was very important, and they also made baskets, pegs and other things needed by rural people, who were deprived of shopping facilities except at infrequent fairs. Furthermore, they bred and trained horses which they sold to farmers and crofters, the deal being sealed with nothing more than a spit on the palm and a handshake. They also supplemented their earnings by activities such as pearl-fishing and seasonal work at harvest times. This economic function differentiated them from the tramps or gypsies and made them more welcome in the countryside, though it would be naïve to say that the tinkers did not occasionally supplement legitimate sources of income by begging and other less legal activities. Many travelling people became quite rich as a result of their economic pursuits.

Economic change deprived travellers of their function. The mechanisation of farms reduced the market for horses and likewise the demand for seasonal labour. Better roads and cars and rural shopping distribution networks made the travellers' wares redundant. As their economic role declined, the travellers were forced more and more into the arms of the welfare state – accepting pensions, social security benefits and housing to ease their plight. This happened first in the Lowlands and later in the Highlands, as two wonderful books demonstrate. (See Further Reading, page 158, under 'Tinkers'.)

As Aberdeen expanded, its industries drew their labour almost entirely from the surrounding farmland and fishing communities. Many came willingly to the town for a better paid and more varied life, but one group never reconciled itself to urban existence and endeavoured to maintain its contacts with the countryside. This was the travelling people, who, as their rural economic role declined, were forced to spend part of the year in Aberdeen, often working in the worst paid jobs and living in the poorest housing, and longing for the day when they could go 'on the road' again. In the works of Stanley Robertson, the incredible richness and pathos of the lives of the travelling people of the North East has been rescued from slipping into oblivion. In his *Fish Hooses*, Stanley records the life of this sub-proletariat in the hellholes of the Aberdeen fish industry in the 1950s, where many travellers found employment. Stanley himself spent a working life of over 30 years in the Aberdeen fish industry. In *Exodus to Alford*, he records the travellers' walking in and out of Aberdeen in the summer months. This book is the nearest we have to a Scottish *Canterbury Tales*, taking a circular route enlivened by adventure and storytelling to Alford and back, *Up the Dee and Doon the Don*. This phrase was the title of a collection of songs by Stanley's aunt, the great Scots singer Jeannie Robertson, who took to the road every summer pre-war.

The travelling people used to live in areas of council housing in Aberdeen called Powis and Sandilands, which as a teenager I thought were slums, till I saw Possil and Blackhill in Glasgow. During the War, Robertson had lived with his family in Powis while his father was with the Gordon Highlanders, but in the summer of 1946 they left the city to take in the flax harvest at Alford. Having had bitter experiences of school and other children, Robertson recalls that he was not sorry to leave the 'scaldies', as the town-dwellers were known, and head for the countryside. The front door of their house was left unlocked and they loaded their possessions – pots, blankets and clothes – onto a horse and cart. They met up with several other travelling families and headed out of the city in an 'Exodus' to the promised land, 'my father like Moses', as Robertson recalls. While the small children rode on the cart, the men and womenfolk walked, chatting and smoking until they reached the first night's stop at Echt, west of Aberdeen. Camp was set up round a fire, and music and storytelling began. The next camp was at Lumphanan, and the third at Alford itself. This was a distance of about 30 miles in three stages, so the travellers were clearly not in any great hurry. At each stop wonderful tales were told, many of which record walking feats in the itinerants' lives.

Having done their harvesting at Alford the travellers moved on, camping and storytelling at fireside halts. They walked to Aboyne, Tarland, Strathdon, Corgarff and Braemar, heading down Deeside past Ballater, Dinnet, Midmar and Garlogie, and arriving at the final camp at Kingswells outside Aberdeen to a wild ceilidh which lasted all night, accompanied by sad thoughts of returning to the city to winter and work. Their summer walk had not been too arduous – about 200 miles all told. Read Stanley Robertson's tales, and listen to the songs of his aunt Jeannie, regretting only that you can no longer hear them by campfire. The tradition of the *Up the Dee and Doon the Don* is no more.

Because of the geographical isolation and economic backwardness of the Highlands, the travellers' role in economic life there lasted longer than in Lowland areas. As a boy on a 1,000 mile cycle ride through the Highlands in the early 1960s, I can recall seeing quite a few tinkers on the road or at camp. Even then their skills as horse dealers and their commercial articles were still needed in an area that the consumer revolution had yet to reach. Tinker families, which took the names of the Highland clans, existed all over the Highlands and tended to have their own special area. Sutherland was the hunting ground of the Stewarts, who for generations had tramped its roads for six months each year, trading with the local people. Latterly they travelled the road north to Tongue from Lairg via

Altnaharra, and also that westwards up Glen Oykell to Assynt, or by Loch Shin to Kinlochbervie and Durness. Though these routes are now surfaced and numbered roads, the Stewarts' ancestors had travelled them before they were even drove roads.

Year after year they returned to the same campsites where grass, water and shelter awaited them. At the sites the bow-tent was raised; a big stout structure, easy to put up and take down. Over a ribcage of pre-bent hazel sticks, a tarpaulin (or skin, or latterly a plastic sheet) was stretched, weighted by stones and surrounded by a drainage ditch. While elsewhere tinkers adapted to all sorts of shapes and sizes of tent, the possibly prehistoric bow-tent remained until the end in Sutherland. At the camp the travellers bought and sold to locals, told stories as old as history, played music and socialised round a campfire (or a stove). Between camps they walked. The tent and poles were placed on the cart with goods for sale and the old and infirm, the cart being led by an adult, usually male. He would be on foot and the other able-bodied members of the family walked behind (or went out selling to isolated houses as they walked), or ahead to prepare camp in the stunningly beautiful landscape.

The Sutherland travellers wintered at Remarstaig outside Lairg, where they built houses of brick and mortar (or wood) with tin roofs. There was the luxury of a dry toilet and even latterly a radio driven by accumulators. The site may have been chosen a century ago because it was by the railway and the railway workers threw great lumps of coal off the trains for the travellers. At Ullapool the fishermen on the quay gave liberally to the travellers of their fish catch, and even the aristocracy were their benefactors. When the Westminsters were at Achfarry the travellers would be sent sides of venison from the estate. Crofters were pleased to see them for the gossip and fun they brought, as much as for their trading.

In the 1950s Hamish Henderson travelled with the Stewart clan recording their tales and songs, especially those of their blind patriarch, the deeply religious Ailidh Dall, a Sutherland Homer. From Ailidh (Alexander) Stewart, Henderson recorded songs and stories 1,000–1,500 years old. However, this was the time when roads into the Highlands were being improved, and the products of the world were penetrating the glens:

> In the fifties plastic came in, cars, buses, Fergie-tractors came – one tractor could be made to serve a whole community! That was good for the crofters but bad for us. Our business was horses, and tin and bringing in what the people couldn't get out to get! In the fifties our business went downhill so fast you couldn't see the smoke!

By the time Timothy Neat interviewed the remaining travellers in the 1990s they were all settled, the last season's tramp with horse and cart and a bow-tent having been undertaken in 1978. Though today's travellers may do a bit of pearl-fishing or other work, they mainly travel for pleasure or to escape harassment, and their battered caravans and cars indicate that they walk the roads no longer.

And in that default the travelling people are merely the last in the long line of pilgrims, soldiers, drovers, distillers and others who have gone before them over 20 centuries. Following in the footsteps of those who walked for necessity is one way of maintaining the organic linkage with the past, and hopefully this work will have interested its readers enough to make them want to go out and do just that. Sadly though, the travellers' routes are now all tarred and traffic-choked, and their footsteps are the only ones in this book I would not recommend the reader to tread.

Addendum

AS STATED EARLIER in this chapter, the Scottish tinkers, and the gypsies or Romany people, are quite distinct, although over time there has been an intermingling to some extent between them, and between both groups and the general population. But whilst the tinkers are indigenous to Scotland, the gypsies, or Egyptians as they were initially known, arrived in the country about 500 years ago. They ranged far but were mainly concentrated in Southern Scotland, from Galloway to the Borders, and especially in the town of Kirk Yetholm in Roxburghshire, which became in some sense their capital.

In 1540 John Faw, the self-styled 'king' of the gypsies actually signed a treaty with King James V of Scotland, pledging allegiance to the king, in return for being given recognition of his own rights: 'In executioun of justice upon his cumpany and folkis, conforme to the lawis of Egipt, and in punissing all thaim that rebellis agains him.' But the gypsy lifestyle, especially their want of Christianity at this time and their habits of stealing, led to a reaction and in the early 17th century they were banished from Scotland under pain of death. This decree was fairly spasmodically enforced, but is probably why the gypsies settled at Kirk Yetholm, which was only a couple of kilometres from England, and whence they could quickly flee into the 'Debateable Lands' of the Scottish-English border, if things became too hot for them.

Many were the routes across the Cheviots even then. A state paper of Henry VIII from the 1540s lists 17 crossings of the range. The gypsies would have got to know them all, both as escape routes and as places where they could ambush and rob passing travellers.

An account of the gyspies in *Blackwoods Magazine* of 1817 gives several accounts of their robberies around the Cheviot, including one concerning Jean Gordon, the original template for the character of Meg Merillees in Walter Scott's novel *Guy Mannering*. On the occasion mentioned, dating from the early 18th century, Jean actually saved a farmer from Kirk Yetholm, who had shown her kindness, from being robbed by the rest of her band. Her own sons – and their wives – were all hanged, however, for sheep stealing. Scott gives the filial number as nine, and their fate as being decided when a sleeping juror at their trial broke the deadlock amongst his peers by waking and shouting, 'Hang them a'!'.

Very gradually the gypsies adopted a more settled life, and some moved into proper houses built at Kirk Yetholm sometime in the 18th century. In the *Old Statistical Account* from the 1790s, the minister notes that there are 50 gypsies in the village, but at the time of the *New Statistical Account* in the 1830s, the Rev. John Baird records that their number has grown to 100. Baird notes that the gypsies are becoming more involved with the Church, and more prone to learn to read and write by the early 19th century, and indeed by the end of the century, when their last 'King' Charles II was crowned in 1898, they had become a tourist attraction and almost entirely given up their old ways of life.

But in the 1830s the gypsies were still travelling, and it is worth quoting Baird's account. The gypsies made tin cups and mugs (hence the term 'muggers') as well as horn spoons and baskets. They also bought in bulk and then resold by piece, cheap earthenware goods. They loaded these in a horse and cart (no colourful gypsy wagon!), and travelled the country-side, living in a rude tent:

> The women carry about the manufactured articles for sale, while the men either remain with the cart or occupy themselves in fishing and poaching, in both of which they are generally expert. The children accompany the females, or collect decayed wood for fuel. At night the whole family sleep under the tent which is generally woollen cloth, and is the same usually that covers their cart during the day. Each family generally travels a particular district, seldom remaining more than a few days in one place... Before autumn all return who are willing and hire themselves as reapers. After harvest work is done, they set off once more to the country, where they continue until the severity of the winter drives them home.

Today in Kirk Yetholm, though doubtless Romany blood still runs in many local veins, the gypsy community has disappeared.

Suggested Walks

WALK 25

Gypsy Rovers: Across the Border and Back (OS 74)

Start in Kirk Yetholm at the memorial to the Gypsies at the foot of High Street (formerly known as Muggers Row, and the home of the gypsy families). Follow the directions to the Pennine Way past the Gypsy Palace, home in the 19th century to Queen Esther Faa Blythe and later King Charles II. Continue on the road over Staerough Hill until the Halter

Burn is crossed, and St Cuthbert's Way is joined, and follow this south of Green Humbleton Hill till the border is reached. Descend through woods to the Elsdon Burn and a couple of miles from the border take the road south to Trowupburn. From here head west along a bridle path which treads north of White Law to reach the border again almost where you crossed it, but with your pursuers given the slip. Descend back to Kirk Yetholm and the pub.

Round trip: 9 miles, 4 hours.

WALK 26

Gypsy Rovers: The Cheviot (OS 74)

Many tales tell of bands of gypsies robbing travellers in the area around the Cheviot, which was criss-crossed by many paths. Today the ascent of this hill from Kirk Yetholm is a well signposted part of the Pennine Way.

A car can be taken from Kirk Yetholm to just short of Burnhead on the Halter Burn. From here the route goes up the glen past Old Halterburnhead and reaches the watershed just south of Black Hag. Thence it goes over the Schill before falling, following the border to the head of College Burn (Refuge Hut). Below you is the dramatic Hen Hole, above is the Cheviot, the ascent of which (optional) is more of a Hell Hole of peat hags and mud. Return by outward route.

Burnhead to the Cheviot summit and return: 15 miles, 8 hours. From Kirk Yetholm, an additional 4 miles in total, 2 hours more.

Places to Visit

These are mainly bad weather options, in addition to the *Suggested Walks* at the end of each chapter.

ROMANS

> Antonine Wall and Bathhouse, Bearsden
> Ardoch Roman Camp, Perthshire
> Hunterian Museum, University of Glasgow

MISSIONARIES

> Iona Abbey
> Isle of Whithorn

PILGRIMS

> St Andrews Cathedral, Fife
> St Duthac's Church, Tain

EARLY TRAVELLERS

> National Library of Scotland, Edinburgh
>   (Project Pont at **www.nls.uk/pont**)
> Culross Palace, Fife
>   (Information on Bruce's mine, visited by Taylor)

JACOBITES AND HANOVERIANS

> Culloden Battlefield and Fort George,
>   both near Inverness
> Glenfinnan Monument, near Fort William
> Ruthven Barracks, near Kingussie

ENGLISH TOURISTS

> Burns' House and Mausoleum, Dumfries

SCIENTISTS

Natural History Museum, University of Aberdeen
(Founded by MacGillivray)

DISTILLERS

Corgarff Castle, Strathdon
(Military anti-smuggling outpost)

WOMEN

Maritime Museum, Aberdeen
Museum of Scottish Country Life, Wester
Kittochside, East Kilbride

IRISH

People's Palace, Glasgow
St Fitticks Kirk, Nigg, Aberdeen
(Graves of Aberdonians killed by Montrose's troops)

TOWN WALKERS

Hielanman's Umbrella, Glasgow Central Station
Carbeth Huts, by Strathblane, Dunbartonshire

TINKERS

Remarstaig ruins, near Lairg, Sutherland
Gypsy Palace, Kirk Yetholm
(View from outside only)

Further Reading

ROMANS
Keppie, Lawrence: *Scotland's Roman Remains* (1998)

PILGRIMS
Yeoman, Peter: *Pilgrimage in Medieval Scotland* (1999)

EARLY TRAVELLERS
Cunningham, I. (ed): *The Nation Survey'd* (2001)
    Essays on Pont
Hume-Brown, P. (ed): *Early Travellers in Scotland* (1891)

JACOBITES AND HANOVERIANS
Reid, Stuart: *Like Hungry Wolves* (1995)
Tabraham, C. and Grove, D.: *Fortress Scotland and the Jacobites*
    (1995)
Woosnam-Savage, R.C.: *1745: Charles Stuart and the Jacobites*
    (1995)

ENGLISH TOURISTS
Walker, C.K.: *Walking North with Keats* (1992)

DROVERS
Haldane, A.R.B.: *The Drove Roads of Scotland* (1973)

SCIENTISTS
Portlock, J.E.: *The Life of Major General Colby* (1869)
    Contains Dawson's account of 1819
Ralph, Robert: *William MacGillivray* (1993)

DISTILLERS
Cooper, Derek: *The Whisky Roads of Scotland* (1981)
    More on the industry than the roads, despite the title.

WOMEN
Smith, Robert: *Grampian Ways* (1980)

IRISH

MacGill, Patrick: *Children of the Dead End* (1914)
As unique as it is moving, a wonderful book.

TOWN WALKERS

Atherton, D. and T. Davies (eds): *Work, Welfare and the Price of Fish; Life in Aberdeen 1925–55* (1995). Hunger marchers

Thomson, I.D.S.: *Jock Nimlin* (1995)

TINKERS

Neat, Timothy: *The Summer Walkers* (1996)

Robertson, Stanley: *Exodus to Alford* (1988)

Robertson, Jeannie: *Up the Dee and Doon the Don* (cassette tape) (1984). Classic North-East ballads

Blackwood's Magazine (1817) 'The Scottish Gypsies'

GENERAL

Kay, Billy (ed): *Odyssey: Voices from Scotland's Recent Past* (1980)
Contains 'From the Gorbals to Gweedore' by Billy Kay, about Irish navvies, and 'Mountain Men' by Ishbel Maclean, about the discovery of the outdoors by the Glasgow unemployed.

Kay, Billy (ed): *Odyssey: the Second Collection* (1982)
Contains 'The Fisher Lassies' by Margaret Bochel, about Nairn girls in Shetland and Great Yarmouth.

'The Lothian Hairst' is reprinted in Ord, John (ed): *Bothy Songs and Ballads* (1990)

'The Donegals' is in McLellan, Robert: *Linmill Stones* (1990)

'The Two Drovers' by Walter Scott is in various editions, originally in the *Waverley Novels*, volume 20.

Some other books published by **LUATH** PRESS

A View from the Ridge

Dave Brown and Ian R. Mitchell

ISBN 1 905222 45 9 PBK £7.50

Winner of Boardman Tasker Prize for Mountain Literature

To some, hill-walking is a physical activity. To others, climbing is all, and everything else is nothing. Because it's not just hills: it's people, characters, fun and tragedy. Every mountaineer will know that it's not just about the anticipation of what hill to climb next, it's a sub-culture of adventure and friendship – all-night card games, monumental hang-overs, storytelling, singing – and above all, free spirits.

In this fitting sequel and essential companion to the classic *Mountain Days and Bothy Nights*, Dave Brown and Ian R. Mitchell capture perfectly the inexplicable desire which brings Scottish hillwalkers back to the mist, mud and midgies every weekend. Their lively, humorous and enthusiastic narrative will revitalise the drive in you to get out on the hills – or you may prefer just to curl up on the couch with this book and a wee dram for company.

If you buy only one mountain book this year make it this 'view from the ridge' and savour its rich, different and fascinating reflections.
KEVIN BORMAN,
High Mountain Magazine

Scotland's Mountains before the Mountaineers

Ian R. Mitchell

ISBN 0 946487 39 1 PBK £9.99

In this ground breaking book, Ian Mitchell tells the story of explorations and ascents in the Scottish Highlands in the days before mountaineering became a popular sport – when Jacobites, bandits, poachers and illicit distillers traditionally used the mountain as sanctuary. *Scotland's Mountains before the Mountaineers* is divided into four Highland regions, with a map of each region showing key summits. While not designed primarily as a guide, it is nevertheless a useful handbook for walkers and climbers. Based on a wealth of new research, this book offers a fresh perspective that will fascinate climbers and mountaineers, and anyone interested in the history of mountaineering, cartography, the evolution of the landscape and the social history of the Scottish highlands.

Who were the first people to 'conquer' Scotland's mountains, and why did they do it?

- Which clergyman climbed all the Cairngorm 4,000-ers nearly two centuries ago?
- How many Munros did Bonnie Prince Charlie bag?
- Which bandit and sheep rustler hid in the mountains while his wife saw off the sheriff officers with a shotgun?

Mountain Days and Bothy Nights

Dave Brown/Ian Mitchell

ISBN 0 946487 15 4 PBK £7.50

Acknowledged as a classic of mountain writing and still in demand ten years after its first publication, this book takes you into the bothies, howffs and dosses on the Scottish hills. Fishgut Mac, Desperate Dan, Stumpy and the Big Yin stalk hill and public house, evading gamekeepers and royalty with a camaraderie which was the trademark of Scots hillwalking in the early days.

As well as being a good read the book is an authentic word picture of this part of the climbing scene in latter-day Scotland, which, like any good picture, will increase in charm over the years.
SCOTTISH MOUNTAINEERING
CLUB JOURNAL

The ideal book for nostalgic hillwalkers and climbers of the 60's, even just the armchair and public house variety... humourous, entertaining, informative, written by two men with obvious expertise, knowledge and love of their subject.
SCOTS INDEPENDENT

Mountain Outlaw

Ian R. Mitchell

ISBN 1 84282 027 3 PBK £6.50

In 1850 Ewan MacPhee, these islands' last outlaw, died awaiting trial in jail in Fort William. This was a man who:

- Had been forced to enlist at the time of the Napoloenic wars, and deserted

- Lived as an outlaw and rustler in Lochaber for over 20 years

- Had several capital offences hanging over his head

- Was a hero to the local peasantry at the time of the Clearances

- Abducted a wife – who became his firmest ally in conflicts with the law

MacPhee has fascinated Ian R. Mitchell for many years. He has sifted the surviving information on the outlaw, examined many of the legends associated with him, bridged the gaps with an imagination of great authenticity, to produce *Mountain Outlaw*, a historical–creative account of MacPhee's life.

(Mitchell's objective was to provide) (..) a compendium of tales that do some justice to Ewan MacPhee. He has not failed in that objective, it is fascinating, indeed, to decide what real and what is less or more so, to separate the fict from the faction, or vice versa. All in all, it's an astounding story, intricately told.
THE DAILY MAIL

This City Now: Glasgow and its working class past

Ian R Mitchell
ISBN 1 84282 082 6 PBK £12.99

This City Now sets out to retrieve the hidden architectural, cultural and historical riches of some of Glasgow's working-class districts. Many who enjoy the fruits of Glasgow's recent gentrification will be surprised and delighted by the gems which Ian Mitchell has uncovered beyond the usual haunts.

An enthusiastic walker and historian, Mitchell invites us to recapture the social and political history of the working-class in Glasgow, by taking us on a journey from Partick to Rutherglen, and Clydebank to Pollokshaws, revealing the buildings which go unnoticed every day yet are worthy of so much more attention.

Once read and inspired, you will never be able to walk through Glasgow in the same way again.

...both visitors and locals can gain instruction and pleasure from this fine volume...Mitchell is a knowledgable, witty and affable guide through the streets of the city...
GREEN LEFT WEEKLY

On the Trail of Queen Victoria in the Highlands

Ian R. Mitchell
ISBN 0 946487 79 0 PBK £7.99

- How many Munros did Queen Victoria bag?
- What 'essential services' did John Brown perform for Victoria? (and why was Albert always tired?)
- How many horses (to the nearest hundred) were needed to undertake a Royal Tour?

What happens when you send a Marxist on the tracks of Queen Victoria in the Highlands? – You get a book somewhat more interesting than the usual run of the mill royalist biographies!

Ian R. Mitchell took up the challenge of attempting to write with critical empathy on the peregrinations of Vikki Regina in the Highlands, and about her residence at Balmoral, through which a neo-feudal fairyland was created on Upper Deeside. The expeditions, social rituals and iconography of that world are explored and exploded from within, in what Mitchell terms a Bolshevisation of Balmorality. He follows in Victoria's footsteps throughout the Cairngorms and beyond, to the further reaches of the Highlands. On this journey, a grudging respect and even affection for Vikki ('the best of the bunch') emerges.

There has never been a book on Victoria like this.

Details of these and all other books published by Luath Press can be found at

www.luath.co.uk

Luath Press Limited
committed to publishing well written books worth reading

LUATH PRESS takes its name from Robert Burns, whose little collie Luath (*Gael.*, swift or nimble) tripped up Jean Armour at a wedding and gave him the chance to speak to the woman who was to be his wife and the abiding love of his life. Burns called one of 'The Twa Dogs' Luath after Cuchullin's hunting dog in Ossian's *Fingal*. Luath Press was established in 1981 in the heart of Burns country, and is now based a few steps up the road from Burns' first lodgings on Edinburgh's Royal Mile.

Luath offers you distinctive writing with a hint of unexpected pleasures.

Most bookshops in the UK, the US, Canada, Australia, New Zealand and parts of Europe either carry our books in stock or can order them for you. To order direct from us, please send a £sterling cheque, postal order, international money order or your credit card details (number, address of cardholder and expiry date) to us at the address below. Please add post and packing as follows: UK – £1.00 per delivery address; overseas surface mail – £2.50 per delivery address; overseas airmail – £3.50 for the first book to each delivery address, plus £1.00 for each additional book by airmail to the same address. If your order is a gift, we will happily enclose your card or message at no extra charge.

Luath Press Limited
543/2 Castlehill
The Royal Mile
Edinburgh EH1 2ND
Scotland
Telephone: 0131 225 4326 (24 hours)
Fax: 0131 225 4324
email: sales@luath.co.uk
Website: www.luath.co.uk